how to be better at....

creativity

THE INDUSTRIAL SOCIETY

The Industrial Society stands for changing people's lives. In nearly eighty years of business, the Society has a unique record of transforming organisations by unlocking the potential of their people, bringing unswerving commitment to best practice and tempered by a mission to listen and learn from experience.

The Industrial Society's clear vision of ethics, excellence and learning at work has never been more important. Over 10,000 organisations, including most of the companies that are household names, benefit from corporate Society membership.

The Society works with these and non-member organisations, in a variety of ways—consultancy, management and skills training, in-house and public courses, information services and multi-media publishing. All this with the single vision—to unlock the potential of people and organisations by promoting ethical standards, excellence and learning at work.

If you would like to know more about the Industrial Society please contact us.

The Industrial Society
48 Bryanston Square
London
W1H 7LN
Telephone 0171 262 2401

The Industrial Society is a Registered Charity No. 290003

how to be better at....

creativity

Geoffrey Petty

KOGAN PAGE

The Industrial Society

YOURS TO HAVE AND TO HOLD
BUT NOT TO COPY

First published in 1997

Kogan Page Limited
120 Pentonville Road
London N1 9JN

© Geoffrey Petty, 1997

British Library Cataloguing in Publication Data
A CIP record for this book is available from the British Library.

ISBN 0 7494 2167 3

Typeset by Intype London Ltd
Printed and bound in Great Britain by Clays Ltd, St Ives plc

ACKNOWLEDGEMENTS

I have talked with very many people about their approach to creative work and learned much from them, but I would like to thank particularly: Trish O'Hare, Brian Petty, Zach Griffey, Susie Tooby, Gurmukh Singh, Sue Moylan, Paul Whitby and Richard Boulton. Most thanks go to Liz Singh who has been my most insightful and tireless critic, and my most supportive and precious friend.

This book is dedicated to all those who struggle to make reality respond to their vision, in the hope it may make their vision brighter, and reality less obstinate.

CONTENTS

Throughout the book the following icons have been used:

tool

activity

reflection activity

HOW TO BE A BETTER . . . SERIES

Whether you are in a management position or aspiring to one, you are no doubt aware of the increasing need for self-improvement across a wide range of skills.

In recognition of this and sharing their commitment to management development at all levels, Kogan Page and the Industrial Society have joined forces to publish the How to a Better . . . series.

Designed specifically with your needs in mind, the series covers all the core skills you need to make your mark as a high-performing and effective manager.

Enhanced by mini case studies and step-by-step guidance, the books in the series are written by acknowledged experts who impart their advice in a particular way which encourages effective action.

Now you can bring your management skills up to scratch *and* give your career prospects a boost with the How to be a Better . . . series!

Titles available are:
How to be Better at Giving Presentations
How to be a Better Problem Solver
How to be a Better Interviewer
How to be a Better Teambuilder
How to be Better at Motivating People
How to be a Better Decision Maker

Forthcoming titles are:
How to be a Better Negotiator
How to be a Better Project Manager
How to be a Better Communicator

Available from all good booksellers. For further information on the series, please contact:

Kogan Page
120 Pentonville Road
London N1 9JN
Tel: 0171 278 0433
Fax: 0171 837 6348

Part I

What is creativity?

1

UNDERSTANDING CREATIVITY

Most people believe that being creative is what a few gifted artists, inventors or entrepreneurs do very occasionally. In fact we are all creative every day. Whenever a problem is solved or a difficulty overcome, whenever something new is made or something old adapted, creativity has been at work. But being creative is difficult.

To maximise your creative potential you must understand the puzzling nature of the creative process. Gifted people discover this intuitively, but everyone can learn it.

You must learn to recognise the six phases in the creative process, so that you can adopt the appropriate mind-set for each. The necessary switches of attitude are alarming. Sometimes you must be playful, uncritical and free. Sometimes you must be strategic, critical and controlled. Sometimes you must be highly rational, while at other times you must rejoice in irrationality. If this sounds daunting there are plenty of tools to help you. When you know how to use the tools that suit you, and which mind-set to use when, then you will begin to discover just how creative you can be.

There are several myths surrounding creativity. Creative ideas are not the products of lightning flashes of inspiration. History shows that in every domain they are the outcome of persistent effort and steady improvement. Creativity does not require huge intelligence. Research shows that the most creative people in any profession are not cleverer than their colleagues. They just know how to get ideas, choose the right ones and how to work these to completion. This completed work may impress and astonish their colleagues, but not the creative workers, for they know it was only the harvest of carefully focused imagination, hard work and steady improvement.

Creative people are at the growing tip of humanity. They deliver the future at work, in the home and at play. Our entire human environment, both its visible and its invisible aspects, is the product of the creative imagination. This would be enough to recommend a careful study of the creative process, but there is more.

Exercising your creative muscle can be a hugely rewarding part of your life. It is a route to self-fulfilment and to happiness. For some it can become even more than this. While many people look fruitlessly for a meaning to their lives outside themselves, many find it within themselves. They make a meaning to their lives by being creative in the area they see as of supreme importance. If they succeed, even in a small way, they have followed their passions, and taken control. And in making their unique contribution, they have begun to discover who they are and what they are for.

Creative action is one of life's greatest challenges, and so one of its greatest rewards. So why not learn how to do it? A mind and a life are terrible things to waste.

2

THE CREATIVE PROCESS

The creative process consists of the following six phases: inspiration, clarification, distillation, perspiration, evaluation and incubation. During a particular piece of creative work each phase should be experienced many times, in no definite order, sometimes for a very short time. The first letter of each phase can be arranged to spell 'icedip'.

We will now take a quick, introductory look at these six icedip phases. Remember that the order of the phases is not significant. More detail, advice and techniques for each phase will be given in later chapters.

In this book I use the term 'creative' in the widest possible sense, to include the creative arts but also invention, design, problem solving, entrepreneurial initiatives and so on.

THE 'ICEDIP' PHASES

Inspiration
In which you generate a large number of ideas

This is the research or idea-generation phase. The process is uninhibited and characterised by spontaneity, experimentation, intuition and risk-taking.

Many people wonder where creative people find their good ideas. The answer is, in among a huge pile of bad ones. Creativity is like mining for diamonds, as most of what you dig is thrown away, but that doesn't make the digging a waste of time. If you 'can't think of anything', you are having difficulty with this inspiration phase, perhaps because you are too self-critical, or expect good ideas to come too quickly.

In the field of the creative arts the inspiration phase is often associated with a search for an individual voice, and with an attempt to conjure up deep feelings of (for example) empathy, spirituality or an intense identification with the subject matter.

This is not a phase in which to be negative or worried about form, practicality, rhyme or quality. For reasons to be examined later you should be rejecting at least 90 per cent of your initial ideas. Let yourself off the leash! If most of the ideas you create are workable, then you didn't take enough risks.

Clarification
In which you focus on your goals

Key questions to ask are:

❑ What am I trying to achieve here?
❑ What am I trying to say?
❑ What exactly is the problem I am trying to solve?
❑ What do I want the finished work to be like?

And, in more open-ended work:

❑ How could I exploit the ideas I have had?
❑ Where could this idea take me—what could I make of it?

The aim here is to clarify the purpose or objective of the work. It is easy to lose your sense of direction while dealing with detailed difficulties in creative work. So you need occasionally to disengage from these obstacles and ask: 'What exactly am I trying to do?'

If you 'get stuck' in the middle of a project, then, rather than dreaming up a stream of alternatives, you need to clarify where exactly you want to go. How to get there is then often straightforward, or even blindingly obvious.

Clarification gets you out of the mire, but it is also required when, say, an artist or designer agonises between two or more equally attractive approaches. Such decisions require a clear sense of purpose.

If you feel lost, stuck, bogged down, confused or uncertain about how to proceed, then clarification is what you need. In this clarification phase you have your eye on the ball, you are being strategic and logical, and focusing on how the finished work will look.

Distillation
In which you look through the ideas you have generated and try to determine which ones to work on

Here, ideas from the inspiration phase are sifted through, usually in the light of the findings of a clarification phase. The best ideas are chosen for further development, or they can be combined into even better ideas.

Distillation is a self-critical phase. It requires cool analysis and judgement, rather than slap-happy spontaneity. However, it should not be so critical as to inhibit productivity entirely. Remember, the ideas you have had are only ideas, not complete solutions—you must not expect too much of them. It is where the ideas can take you that counts, not the ideas themselves.

Perspiration
In which you work determinedly on your best ideas

This is where the real work is done. You are involved in determined and persistent effort towards your goal, and you will usually be involved in further inspiration, distillation and clarification phases.

Evaluation
In which you look back over your work in progress

In the evaluation phase you examine your work for strengths and weaknesses. Then you need to consider how the work could be improved, by removing weaknesses but also by capitalising on its strengths. Then there will probably need to be another perspiration phase to respond positively to the suggestions for improvement. Perspiration and evaluation phases often alternate to form a cycle.

Hardly anyone gets things perfect first time. Creative people adapt to improve. Many people dislike the evaluation phase at first. However, highly creative people are nearly always inveterate revisers. They tinker with work that would make others gape in delight. Actually this evaluation phase can be very rewarding, and no work of real merit will be produced without it. If Shakespeare and Picasso found they had to revise their efforts, then I expect even you will need to!

Incubation
In which you leave the work alone, though you still ponder about it occasionally, leaving it 'on the surface of your mind'

Many brilliant ideas have occurred in the bath or in traffic jams. If you are able to stop work on a project for a few days, perhaps to work on other things, this will give your subconscious mind time to work on any problems encountered, and will also distance you somewhat from your ideas so that you are better able to evaluate them.

Incubation is particularly useful after an inspiration or a perspiration phase, or if a problem has been encountered. Creative people are often surprisingly patient and untidy, and are content to let half-baked ideas, loose ends and inconsistencies brew away in their subconscious until 'something turns up'.

Whenever Sir Isaac Newton had a particularly thorny problem he always worked on it just before he went to sleep. He said, 'I invariably woke up with the solution'.

Those are the six phases of the creative process. In contrast to this complex, multi-phased process, 'uncreative' people, though they may have the skills necessary for original work, will tend to latch on to the very first idea that comes to them, and complete the work quickly and uncritically, without revision, and without serious thought about what they were trying to achieve.

The first letters of these six phases can be arranged to spell 'icedip' which may help you to remember them. Remember though, that each of these 'icedip' phases should be encountered many times, sometimes for very short periods, and not necessarily in any particular sequence.

> You need to adopt the right phase at the right time. For example, no amount of distillation can help you if you need clarification. Many creative blocks are due to the determined adoption of an inappropriate phase. So if stuck . . . switch phases!

When you are involved in your creative work, do you make good use of each phase and use each phase as often as you should? Techniques to help you work effectively in each of these phases will be provided in later chapters.

MIND-SETS

One of the main difficulties for creative people is that the different phases require radically different, even opposite 'mind-sets', each of which is difficult to sustain without deliberate effort. These are outlined below.

Inspiration   In order to generate a large number of different ideas you need to be deeply engrossed, fearless and free: spontaneous, risk-taking, joyful, 'slap-happy', intuitive and improvisational.

It is very common instead to be self-conscious and fearful, and to try to use inappropriate logical thinking. There is also a common tendency to accept your first decent idea, instead of exploring more fully.

Clarification   In order to clarify what you are trying to achieve you need to be strategic, unhurried, logical and clear-minded, and not afraid to ask difficult questions.

Many people fail to clarify; they fail to achieve their goals because they don't know what they are.

Evaluation In order to improve earlier work you need to be critical, positive and willing to learn: self-critical (ruthlessly so sometimes), but positive about your vision of how the work could be, and your ability to do this. You must see weaknesses as opportunities to improve, and to learn.

Instead, creative people often see criticism as a threat, and so fail to improve their work, and to learn.

Distillation In order to choose your best ideas from the inspiration phase you need to be positive, strategic and intrepid: judgemental, but optimistic about where each idea might take you. Be clear about where you want the ideas to take you, and daring enough to take on original ideas. You need to be realistic but ready to take on challenges.

Common mistakes are to choose ideas which are familiar and well worked out, instead of those that will best achieve your intentions.

Incubation In order to leave ideas for your subconscious to work on you need to be unhurried and trusting. You must expect difficulties, trust yourself to find a way round them and not be panicked into adopting a weak solution.

Few people realise that some ideas take time to hatch, and see difficulties and indecision as a sign of failure.

Perspiration In order to bring your ideas to fruition you need to be uncritical, enthusiastic and responsive. You need to be positive and persistent, deeply committed and engaged, and ready to respond positively to any shortcomings.

It is common for even very creative people not to make the best of this phase. They are often uncertain and self-critical, and see weaknesses as lack of talent, instead of as a need for more work or a different approach.

The creative person needs to switch continually between these radically different, and difficult, mind-sets. This requires enormous flexibility as some mind-sets are almost the exact opposite of each other. In the inspiration phase you need to be uncritical, risk-taking and subjective, but in the clarification phase you need to be critical, careful and objective. If you use an inappropriate mind-set you are in deep trouble: you will not get many original ideas if you are critical, careful and strategic, and you will not clarify your purpose effectively if you are slap-happy and uncritical.

Most people find they are stronger in some phases than in others, perhaps because our personality often gives us a predominant mind-set. Some people have masses of ideas, but little idea how to work them to a successful conclusion. Others have difficulty getting the ideas on which to exercise their persistence, skills and good judgement.

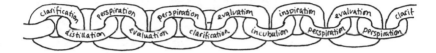

The icedip chain

A given piece of creative work involves a long chain of the icedip phases, each phase being revisited many times. But a chain is only as strong as its weakest link. You need to know your weakest phases, and the techniques and mind-sets which will help you make them stronger. There are some simple strategies which can hugely improve your performance, even in your strongest phases, though these will take practice if you want to make the best of them. A better understanding of each phase, along with its tools and mind-set, will help avoid those blocks and frustrations which prevent you performing to the best of your ability. You will find advice on each phase in Chapters 4 to 10 of this book.

But first it is important to realise what creative thinking is *not*!

WHY LOGICAL THINKING IS NOT ENOUGH

Here is a challenge. You are to attach a candle to a wall, with only the candle, a book of matches and a box of drawing pins. How would you do it? Think of a solution before reading on.

The challenge

Researchers found that people who are given this problem usually adopt one of two approaches.

The first group start by lighting the candle with the matches and then attempting to glue the candle to the wall with molten wax. Then they find the wax runs down the wall instead of staying where they put it. The challenge has changed into a problem. How do I build up the wax in one place? Then perhaps they use the book of matches to stop the wax running down the wall. But then they find the wax is not strong enough to hold the candle. The problem has changed. How do you make the candle less heavy? . . .

The other group try to pin the candle to the wall with the drawing pins, but the candle is too thick for the drawing pins. The challenge is again displaced by a problem, on which all attention is focused. They shave the candle down with one of the pins. Then they find the candle splits when the pin is driven in. The problem has changed. How do you strengthen the split candle? Perhaps with molten wax? . . .

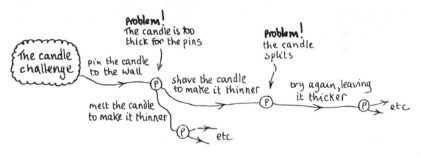

Step by step thinking

The approach is to leap on a likely strategy, such as pinning the candle to the wall, and then move from problem to problem along decision-making branches like those shown in the figure above. The situation is rather like that of a rat in a maze.

There is an unexamined assumption behind this strategy— that an ideal solution waits at the end of the chain of problems. This is often not the case. The rat may be in the wrong part of the maze.

People adopt this 'rat tracking' strategy because they don't have an alternative, or because they feel secure and purposeful when using step-by-step sequential thinking. Sometimes, of course, this way of thinking works, which is why we use it. It is a very effective strategy if the challenge is similar to one that you have been successful with before. But it is a very ineffective strategy if you have:

❑ a novel challenge
❑ a complex situation
❑ a need for your very best ideas
❑ a need for originality.

In these cases you cannot rely on deduction from prior experience. You need to use creative thinking or inductive techniques such as the 'creative leap'.

The creative leap involves guessing an approach or a solution, and then using logic or some other test to see whether this guess will work. If this 'hindsight' suggests that the solution is a good one, then all is well. If, as is more likely, the guess will not work then you adapt the guess or try a completely new one. In this way the whole maze is briefly explored in the hope of chancing on a solution.

If that sounds haphazard, that's because it is! You have only intuition, skill and luck to guide you, and an effective idea may take some time to find. However, the next chapter will give you

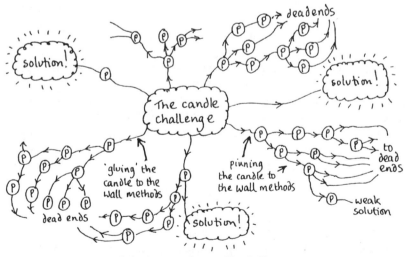

Solutions to the candle challenge

tools and strategies that will greatly increase your ability to generate creative ideas, and by the end of it you will have no difficulty in providing some elegant solutions for the candle challenge.

It is important to appreciate that although creative ideas are logical in hindsight they cannot be arrived at logically. Look at the diagram and imagine you are working on the candle challenge. If you rat track outwards, you cannot know in advance which branch or which turn will take you to the best solution. Will gluing with wax work? Will pinning the candle to the wall work? To make matters worse the diagram is in fact a considerable simplification, as in reality there is an infinity of possible solutions, only some of which will work well in practice. So even if you could explore the entire maze in a detailed, step-by-step manner, it would take you for ever!

What stunts creativity more than any other factor is the common belief that you can best meet challenges, solve problems and generate new designs by the skilled use of logical thinking, that is, by moving from the centre of the above figure to the edge. In fact you must make creative leaps to the edge, and then see if you can work your way back to the reality of the challenge. This means you will be thinking from your guessed solution back to the challenge, instead of the other way round.

The step-by-step improvement of an apparently promising solution may not lead to the best solution, indeed it may not lead to a solution at all. We must start thinking in the opposite direction. How do we do that? There are several approaches, both systematic and poetic, and we will look at them in detail now.

Part II

The icedip phases
The creative process in detail

INSPIRATION

The *inspiration* phase is an uncritical search for ideas. The process is usually uninhibited and spontaneous, and plenty of risks are taken. It is experimental and exploratory, and the aim is to unleash your imagination rather than to generate the perfect solution. However, an inspiration phase can be focused in a very logical and systematic way, as Chapter 6 on clarification, makes clear.

In the field of the creative arts the inspiration phase often involves an inner search for deep feelings associated with the subject matter, and in finding this personal response, one may find an individual and original voice.

QUANTITY NOT QUALITY

We saw in Chapter 3 that problems which require creativity cannot be solved like a sum. There is no logical path to a quick solution, so be patient with yourself. You will get a load of bad ideas before you get any good ones. When you are digging for diamonds most of what you mine is rubbish, but digging out this rubbish is not a waste of time. It has been said that 99 per cent of all new ideas are garbage, regardless of the domain in which you are working. So you need to be prolific as well as patient.

It would be an error to suppose that the great discoverer seizes at once upon the truth, or has any unerring method of divining it. In all probability the

*errors of the great mind exceed in number those of the less vigorous one.
Fertility of imagination and abundance of guesses at the truth are among
the first requisites of discovery.*

Economist William Jevons

In order to illustrate the idea-generating techniques described
below I will use the candle problem described in Chapter 3. I
will also look at another problem based on a true story.

The lift problem

A large company in London is housed in an eight-storey office
building with only two lift shafts. For some time the managing
director has had a nagging problem; his employees keep complaining about the length of time they have to wait for a lift.
Consequently he has asked for quotes from engineering companies for the installation of a new lift shaft.

Two quotes have arrived, one for around £7m for an extra lift
shaft and three for about £1m for faster lifts in the existing
shafts. But one quote has arrived from an engineer who says he
could solve the problem for £60,000. This quote was rejected
out of hand at first, but the director was intrigued. Finally he
telephoned and asked: 'How can you fit a lift shaft for £60,000?'

The cheap solution the engineer described still works well to
this day. What was it? See if you can find the answer to this and
the candle problem using the 'inspiration' techniques described
below. But first of all you might like to try to generate some
ideas without them.

IMPROVISATION

Improvisation is a free-flowing exploration best carried out with
full confidence and enthusiasm. It is an uncritical search for,
and experimentation with, ideas. Although an improvisation can
constitute a performance, as in jazz for example, I use the term
exclusively in the sense of an untidy speculative exploration. It

is not a first draft, as this comes much later. It is usually done in private or in a trusted group.

Watch a child playing. He picks up a toy and plays with it for a little. When he feels he has exhausted its possibilities he chucks it down and picks up another. This is how to play with ideas in improvisation. Don't be shy or inhibited, be confident and bold.

Musicians improvise. Artists and designers doodle and sketch; problem solvers and scientists hypothesise or fantasise with 'What would happen if...?' or 'How about trying...?'. All creative people improvise. But why?—The answer is because ideas hardly ever pop into your head unbidden; you have to go out looking for them.

> John Braine, author of *Room at the Top* suggests, in *Writing a Novel*, that novelists should write for at least three two-hourly sessions a week: 'It isn't that inspiration doesn't exist, but it comes only with writing.'

> *I don't believe in inspiration. I believe in work, because while one works one's creativity is opened.*
>
> Giacomo Manzu, sculptor

But improvising in our blame-ridden culture isn't easy. Most people take their poor ideas as a measure of their inability. This is nonsense. Poor ideas are inevitable; everybody has them. To go back to our mining analogy, you dig out a handful and there are no diamonds. You dig out another and there are still no diamonds. Soon a nagging, negative inner voice says: 'You are a lousy diamond finder'.

How should you reply? By saying: 'Give me a chance! I have to look in places where diamonds aren't in order to find where they are!' When improvising we all have a version of this nagging censor within us which says 'that's a bad idea'. This censor needs silencing. It does not understand that most ideas are bound to be bad, that is the nature of the inspiration phase, even for the most talented.

> *The chances are that, in the course of his lifetime, the major poet will write more bad poems than the minor, simply because major poets 'write a lot'.*
>
> WH Auden

Improvisation is a hunting process, wading through a lot of bad ideas, because this is the only way of finding the good ones.

> Einstein conducted what he called 'thought experiments' which were really free improvisations. In one, he imagined himself riding on a light beam, and the paradoxes he encountered led him to develop his theory of relativity. Doubtless many of his 'thought experiments' were unproductive, but we never hear about those!

How to improvise

When comedians or actors improvise they are taught always to 'accept' absolutely and uncritically any idea that is given them. If the person they are working with says an elephant has walked into the room—then an elephant has walked into the room! There should be no hesitation or half-heartedness about this acceptance. Musicians also 'accept' uncritically; indeed when 'jamming' together they have little choice but to accept what has just been played. The trick is to accept not only uncritically, but also wholeheartedly, as if it were the best idea you had ever heard. The aim is to remove the constraint placed upon your imagination by self-criticism.

Improvising is often best done in 'real time' (i.e. don't pause for reflection or even allow yourself to hesitate, try to make your improvisations flow naturally). This helps to disable the critical faculties because one is working too quickly for conscious control, and herein lies the power of improvisation for idea generation. It silences the ignorant censor who does not understand diamond mining. Also, 'accepting' forces you down strange alleys you would otherwise never have explored, and you are soon in completely uncharted territory. The extraordinary creative fertility of children owes much to 'accepting' and the absence of the 'internal critic'.

At least in the field of the arts there is often intense emotional commitment. Don't be scared of going 'over the top'. If you never go over the top, your caution will ensure you will never reach it! Caution tends to suck you down those tried and tested rat tracks. Effective artists are all characterised by originality, authentic personal expression, deep emotional communication and being true to themselves. This all requires that you remove inhibition, release your imagination and follow it joyfully until you find the real you.

> Beethoven's improvisations were considered by some of his contemporaries to be better than his compositions. He was so enraged by a trite composition composed by a rival, that immediately after its performance he picked up the cello part, took it to the piano, turned it upside down and used this as the source of an extemporisation which completely dazzled the audience. He eventually reworked this burst of creativity into his third (and some say his finest) symphony. The first few notes of the symphony are still the same as that of the upside down cello part!

Most of your ideas will not work. That's fine. Play with them for a bit then move on to others. The trick is not to worry about the products you are creating but, like a child playing, revel in the process. Enjoy yourself. Eventually, perhaps partly by accident, your exploring and experimenting will begin to reap rewards and you will begin to get ideas. And if you improvise often, in time you will get some really productive ideas, and immediately these will inspire you to even better ones. You will be 'on a roll', locked in the moment, completely absorbed in what you are doing. This is one of life's greatest pleasures—the real joy of creativity.

Even if you get no useful ideas at all, improvisation is still a most valuable activity because:

❑ you practise your skill (practice ensures you remain supple and fluent enough to make good use of your ideas when they finally come)
❑ you learn what doesn't work and evaluation will show why it doesn't work
❑ incubation can use bad ideas to suggest good ones, and
❑ you should have enjoyed yourself!

Improvisation is an excellent technique if you have trouble

getting started with creative work; if you are 'blocked'; if you are bogged down with a project; if you don't know where to start; or if you are just plain terrified. Try some of the techniques described later on in this chapter, and learn to silence your inner censor.

Improvisation sessions

Try three improvisation sessions using the following guidelines.

Play with some ideas in a speculative and playful way—the 'roughs' you produce should not be neat or complete. If you find this hard, try a short, high energy burst of activity. Take risks, turn your critic off and enjoy yourself! The standard of what you produce is irrelevant as you are exploring, and there is no need to make use of anything you produce. Ignore 'errors'. The whole concept of errors is irrelevant: this is not even the first draft and you are not making anything that can be spoiled.

If you hardly ever improvise or are scared of it then remember the following.

❑ Don't let anyone see or hear what you produce.
❑ Never ever criticise your work, or look back over it to correct it. Accept enthusiastically practically every idea you produce until you tire of it and move on to another. If you find this impossible and you want to rework an idea don't do this by correction. Start the imperfect idea again on a 'fresh slate', leaving your original attempt unaltered.
❑ Don't be timid, but be bold, confident and positive.
❑ Work quickly, abandon meticulous attention to detail and work in a rough and ready way.
❑ Avoid 'displacement activities' such as sharpening pencils. Blunt ones will do just fine!
❑ Leave it a day before looking at anything you produced.

If you have real problems with improvisation concentrate on the process and ignore the products of your improvisation sessions entirely.

❏ Tell yourself you are just having a 'warm up' practice in order to improve your skills, not a search for ideas.
❏ Accept defeat in advance: promise not to use any of the ideas you generate. If necessary, burn them all immediately!
❏ Remind yourself that no one has ever died of improvisation. (Though one could argue that many suffer an artistic death from the lack of it.)

This is a very legitimate approach, as most creative people are in need of more practice than they can get from the creation of their more acceptable work, and many artists improvise primarily in order to 'keep their hand in', or increase their skills and fluency.

Only a mediocre writer is always at his best.

W Somerset Maugham

Then what? Do it again! Remember, you are rummaging for good ideas among bad ones, and the more bad ones you uncover, the more good ones you are likely to find.

You must throw yourself into the pleasure of play, enjoying the medium for its own sake, doing it your way and not worrying about what others would think about your work.

In the end you may prefer to adopt your own improvisation strategies. That's fine. But be sure they allow you to explore uncritically, and do not allow you to hide from yourself in play-safe strategies.

ADVANCED IMPROVISATION STRATEGIES

When you have the hang of uncritical improvisation then you could try improvising drafts. Very short time scales help to prevent your 'critical self' getting a premature grip on your ideas. For example, set yourself tasks like the following. In the time it takes you to drive to work, or to wash up, you will: think of three ways of increasing the efficiency of the sales office; or produce an outline for a short story; or think of three new approaches to pencil shading; or think of three possible solutions to that nagging problem in your present piece of work.

Creative bursts

Taking this idea further you could set aside half an hour a day to 'quantity bagging'. Make yourself write two poems or paint two paintings in half an hour. If you do this for a week or two some ideas will begin to suggest themselves.

But . . . how should I start?

It doesn't matter what your first idea is because it's unlikely to be useful anyway; good ideas tend to come in the middle or at the end of an improvisation session. So start wherever you like— tell yourself you are just warming up.

But . . . how will I find time?

One doesn't find this time, one makes it! You can think speculatively at any time. You can do it in the bath or on the way to work. It's a habit of mind. But you will need time for dedicated improvisation sessions or creative bursts.

But . . . what if my ideas are all awful?

Then read this section on improvisation again . . . of course your ideas will be awful!

Try to improvise often, because a constant stream of indifferent ideas is the only route to the brilliant ones. At least for those involved in the creative arts, improvisation allows you to get in touch with the real you, and to become what you could be, with your own unique taste, with your subconscious, with your artistic soul; it is perhaps the only way to free the spirit and to develop your original voice.

You may find it helpful at first to have something to improvise on. This is the subject of the next few pages.

Creativity and humour

When using analogy and other idea generating techniques there is a strong tendency to get sidetracked into the humorous aspects of the suggestions generated. Arthur Koestler showed that creativity is very close to humour, because both humorous and creative ideas are unexpected, yet logical in hindsight. For example:

Waiter: 'I'm sorry we don't serve hippies.'
Hippy: 'That's OK, I don't eat them.'
or

Headmaster: 'Jones! Being a clown will never pay the bills.'
Jones: That's right sir, have you ever thought of window cleaning?'

Often, with both creativity as with humour, we experience a 'paradigm shift', meaning that we suddenly see familiar material in a new way. When this new penny drops, we experience that delightful 'Eureka!' feeling, and often laugh. So, if some of the ideas you create are comical it's a good sign, meaning you are able to see the old material in a new way. It certainly does not mean your ideas are worthy of contempt. So don't let the discovery of silly ideas undermine your confidence.

However there is often at least one person in a group who hijacks a serious creative session by turning it into a search for jokes, instead of a search for ideas. If others you work with cannot be made to understand that silly or comical ideas are inevitable, but not to be searched for, then you may need to work without them, at least in this 'inspiration' phase.

Improvisation questionnaire

Are you good at improvising? Answer the questionnaire below after a few improvisation sessions

                                    Yes!! Yes No No!!
1. Did you enjoy the sessions?
2. Were many of the ideas poor?
3. Did you have any downright silly ideas?
4. Did you manage to keep working during the session?
5. Did you manage to remain uncritical?

6. Were you being genuinely experimental
   and exploratory?

Yes!! = 2 Yes = 1 No = 0 No!! = –1.

SCORE: For each of the six questions above, score as follows:

Improving your improvisation technique

If you have scored above eight in the questionnaire you are doing well. But aim for a top score by answering the following questions.

What do you find most difficult about improvisation? Examine the questionnaire items you scored badly on. Plan how you might overcome this difficulty, perhaps using some experimentation. Read back over the 'how to improvise' check-list on page 34–5. Did you keep to it?

Remember that if you play safe you will tend to stick to well-tried and tested (that is unoriginal) strategies. It takes most people a long time to develop an improvisatory style that is both widely exploratory and useful in generating ideas. Don't expect instant results.

INSPIRATION TOOLS

You will experience an initial reluctance to use these tools. As always when learning new techniques you will be awkward and ineffective to begin with, but patient practice will allow you to master them. Try each tool separately, say three times, with ten minutes for each trial. They are exhausting to use, perhaps because one so often draws a blank. Work with real commitment, starting with the tools that attract you most, then moving on to the harder ones. The advanced tools may need more effort. Beware of the 'I'm too clever to need these tools' syndrome; however clever you are, the tools will make you better.

Association and movement

To set this idea in context I will take as an example a creative writing session. But the technique has wider application, and you will see it being used time and time again with the other inspiration techniques mentioned below. Imagine a writer working on a passage to do with the sea. She writes down words associated with *spray,* and then words suggested by this association and so on. This creates chains of association like this.

```
Spray ──► aerosol ──► spray painting ──► vandals ...
      ──► white flecks ──► dandelion seeds ──► dandelion clock ...
      ──► spittle ──► spitting ──► anger ──► rage ──► violence ...
      ──► spray of flowers ──► bouquet ──► wedding ──► catching bride's bouquet
      ──► shower ──► umbrella ──► rain ...
      ──► droplets ──► tears ──► cry ...
```

Chains of association

This is done *without any preconceptions about whether or how these ideas might be used.* While thinking of the next word in the chain, try to forget the initial word 'spray', or the original subject of the sea, and concentrate on the latest word in the chain. This can all be done mentally or on paper.

Many people suggest that you should work quickly and without much thought, so that the associations come unedited from your subconscious. Others counsel a more careful approach. Try both approaches and discover which suits you.

The more distant associations can be used in more poetic writing:

an **angry** sea, **spitting** its **spray** into my eyes . . .'. Closer associations create a more prose-like style:

'He watched the wind-blown **flecks** of **spray** . . .'.

Association is not the exclusive preserve of writers. If you look for it, you will find the 'poetic logic' of association in every field of the creative arts. This is no coincidence, as our mind works by associative connections. This is why the technique is so powerful and so widely applicable. It is often used with all the subsequent tools as you will see.

Analogy

This technique is best explained by example. Think of the lift problem described on page 30: we need to reduce waiting time for the lifts in an office block. What is the general sort of problem to which this belongs? It is a transport problem.

We have now stepped up a logical level from the particular (lift) to the general (transport). Now we step down again by asking ourselves what other sorts of solutions there are to 'trans-

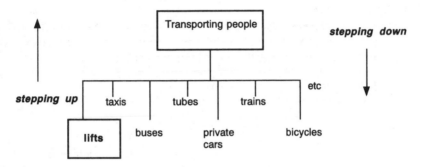

A transport problem

porting people type problems'. We move from the general to the particular and get taxis, buses, trains ... These are all *analogies* for a lift. Now we can mine these analogies for ideas that might speed or reduce the waiting time for the lifts, in the following ways.

If a lift were a train:
❏ an announcer would tell you when it was about to arrive (the arrival of a lift could be announced)
❏ there would be stopping and express lifts (one lift could miss out some floors).

If a lift were a bus:
❏ there would be a timetable telling you at what times past the hour the lift would arrive (the lift could run to a set timetable)
❏ you would be able to see it coming and rush for it ... (a

light could show the position of the lift to anyone on the floor)
❏ there would be times when there was no lift available for, say, the next ten minutes (floors could have times in the hour, e.g. 'half-past until quarter-to', when they could not use the lift).

Try the 'If a lift were a . . .' technique with a taxi and a bicycle before reading on.

If a lift were a taxi:
❏ you could call one up on a telephone whenever you needed it, and it would tell you when it had arrived. You wouldn't need to wait . . . (could you order a lift by telephone?)

If a lift were a bicycle:
❏ Well it would have a bell on it! (a bell could ring to say when the lift was about to arrive)
❏ it would carry you there, under your own steam, whenever you wanted to go (could people use the stairs instead of the lift?)

To make use of analogy we look at the analogous solutions, keeping the original problem also in mind. The 'If a lift were a . . .' starting point helps.

This process will take you off the rat track, but don't just stay where it's dumped you! Use *association* to produce *movement* to new ideas.

The bicycle analogy suggested no directly useful ideas, but it *did* lead to productive trains of thought:

bicycle → bell → bell to say when the lift will arrive

bicycle → pedalling effort → independence → walking up stairs.

After being displaced from the original problem (and the rat tracks), we try to work our way back to the original problem by association.

I have omitted the useless ideas generated by these analogies (the majority of them!) to save space. But you should write all your ideas down however useless they appear. I could see no value in the following when I first wrote it down: 'If a lift were a bus it would have a route with a number'. Later on that day I realised that if lift 'routes' missed out alternate floors this would speed the lift's progress.

We are getting some ideas. Some may be useful, some you might be tempted to reject. For example, using the stairs will not appeal to the lazy or those with a heart complaint. So scrap the idea? No! Never abandon an idea because of an obvious disadvantage, instead overcome the disadvantage.

What if people were encouraged to use the stairs to keep fit? Or paid extra if they used them? What if whole floors in the building had a day of the week when they couldn't use the lift? What if only every alternate floor had a 'lift stop' and only people with heart conditions were allowed to use the 'request stops' in between? (Hang on, 'lift stop' . . . 'request stop'—this is bus vocabulary! Using the analogy of a bus has increased the vocabulary of our ideas.)

Keep thinking of the lift problem as we look at other inspiration techniques. Analogy has given us some interesting ideas, but other techniques will suggest even better ones, as you will see!

> Mark Brunel (the father of Isombard Kingdom Brunel) made the London tube system a technical possibility by learning a revolutionary tunnelling technique from the wood worm.

Close and distant analogies

We could have chosen some very close analogies for a lift, using the small 'step up' to 'lifting people', giving 'escalator', 'rocket' etc. (Can you generate ideas with these?) Above I used the larger step up to 'transporting people' to generate a number of fair ideas. But we could step up still further. What is more general than 'transporting people'? Perhaps 'transporting things'? This gives 'freight', 'letters', 'parcels' . . . etc.

Close analogies are few in number, suggesting workable but sometimes obvious solutions ('rocket' suggests speeding up the lift). There are usually many more very distant analogies, generating mainly unusable, but some original ideas. ('Letters' suggests by association that if the internal post in the building were faster, people would use the lifts less.)

Analogy broadens the focus of your attention and *allows you to look at the problem in a different way*. It gives you a different map for the same territory or a different 'model' for the situation. This paradigm shift can be astonishingly powerful, but like all 'inspiration' techniques analogy often draws a blank.

Using analogy takes practice, especially for those used to problem solving in a highly focused, 'don't change the subject' manner. But creative people get useful ideas because they are able to look at problems in a 'slacker', freewheeling, more relaxed and open way.

Activity

Now use the analogy technique on the candle problem. Remember, you need to fix a candle to a wall with only a book of matches and a box of drawing pins to help you.

Step up first:
What sort of problem is this? It's a 'fix it to the wall' problem.

Step down:
What else is fixed to a wall? Can you mine these analogies for possible solutions? Try this for yourself. My analogies are shown below and the ideas they generate are on page 74. Try it yourself before looking! Most of your ideas will be rubbish, but that's OK! If you work at it, some will astonish you.

Solutions to the candle problem using analogy

'Fix it to the wall' solutions include: picture, shelf, gutter, paint, wallpaper, bracket, coat-hook, curtain rail . . .

I bet you forgot to step up again to 'it's a fixing problem' to give the distant analogies of: hinge, axle, clip, clamp, hook, tenon and other joints, batten, cement, glue . . .

The solutions suggested by these analogies are on page 74.

Examples of the use of analogy

A clothing company found its quality control system was passing imperfect garments.

Step up:
This is a 'sort out the good from the bad' problem.

Step down:
We get analogies like 'sewage filtration' and 'the body's immune system'.

❏ **A sewage filtration plant:** This uses a continuous filter bed system (Could the clothes be gradually inspected, rather than just at the end of the production line? For example, could each worker check the seam sewn by the previous worker?)

❏ **The body's immune system:** White cells kill viruses. Inoculation involves introducing a small sample of dead viruses. The immune system then learns to detect and kill the viruses. (Could faulty garments be deliberately introduced to teach inspectors and to check their performance?) etc.!

The artistic use of analogy

Many artists unconsciously think in analogies, but they can also make conscious use of them. Method acting teaches an actor who wishes to convey menace to pretend that their head and upper body is that of a panther. This may sound silly, but it gets extraordinarily effective results.

We cannot think without analogies, as they are the mental 'maps' which represent the territory of reality. These maps structure our understanding, but they also limit it, because no map is perfect. The maps have errors and omissions, and these limitations restrict our understanding. When the current map is inadequate it is time to go looking for a new one. The crucial realisation is that 'the map is not the territory'. A new map may show us new roads and new connections that were not shown on our old map, enabling us to move around the old territory in a new way.

Searching oblique sources

Search for ideas in an area which is related to your main subject matter, but is not identical. Both close and distant 'relatives' to your main subject matter could be tried. Here is an example. An interior designer working on a kitchen may be expected to browse through kitchen catalogues. But how about the designer looking at catalogues concerning commercial kitchens, hospitals, bathrooms, sitting rooms or offices? Many of the ideas generated will be useless of course, yet some will have immediate applications: mirrors, towel rails, taps, angle-poise lamps etc. Others will be more unusual, for example, sitting rooms might suggest the kitchen has pot plants, bookshelves, a television or hi fi, or even a sofa.

However, this direct cross-fertilisation is not the most powerful use of oblique sources. The main benefit is found by being knocked off the rat track, and then using association to work back towards the main problem. For example, suppose the designer looks in a bathroom catalogue for kitchen ideas and sees a photograph of a shower. Most of us would say 'Can't use that'; many would simply laugh. But watch how association can be used to gain movement from 'showers' towards useful ideas.

Showers → glass doors and curtains → Could the kitchen have a glass door? Or curtains to separate it from the living room? This in turn suggests that there could be a removable partition between the kitchen and the dining room to make more space for dinner parties.

Other times and other countries

An enormously fruitful oblique source for you to research is your area of creative interest in another country, or at another time, or both! The impressionist painters were profoundly influenced by Japanese painters such as Andô Hiroshige. Monet collected many of his prints. Similarly, French *nouvelle cuisine* was brought about by applying Japanese culinary ideas to French cooking.

Picasso was fascinated by African wood carving, while contemporary painters ignored it, thinking it had nothing to do with their art. Then Picasso began painting faces and figures in the symbolic, non-representational style he found in African masks. This abandonment of literal realism created a furious reaction in the art world and started an artistic revolution.

Henry Moore had ancient Mexican figures in his private collection and he was clearly influenced by their rounded simplicity. Stravinsky made overt use of old musical forms in his 'Back to Bach' neoclassical phase. Pop art drew a literal inspiration from comic books. General Norman Schwarzkopf won the Gulf War with a strategy he learned from the 200 BC commander Hannibal. I could fill a book with further examples! There are plenty of original and effective ideas out there, if you only go looking in the 'wrong' place! Be eclectic!

> An expert is someone who knows more and more about less and less until he knows absolutely everything about nothing.

Oblique sources can be copied, but they are more usually mined for ideas, suggestions or radically different approaches. The ideas generated are often extensively developed, so that the source of the inspiration would never be guessed. Who would see the influence of an African mask in a Picasso painting? And who thinks of wood worm when they see a tunnelling machine?

> Writers often use oblique sources: a magazine article about a tidal barrage or a coastguard safety leaflet will suggest more original words or approaches to the sea, and more original story lines, than more direct material.

Darwin reported in his autobiography that he had been trying to develop a new theory of evolution for some time when he happened to read 'for amusement' Malthus's essay on human population. Malthus was not at all concerned with evolution but in drawing attention to the many checks on human population growth such as famine and plague. Darwin realised that this same struggle for existence was experienced by animals and plants, and this led him to the concept of 'the survival of the fittest':

... it at once struck me that under these circumstances ... [famine and plague] favourable variations would tend to be preserved and unfavourable ones to be destroyed ... Here then I had at last got a theory by which to work.

Some 20 years later, but before Darwin had published his ideas, Alfred Wallace independently discovered what is now known as Darwin's theory of evolution, also after reading Malthus's essay!

Philosophers of science such as Kuhn have shown that to create a new scientific theory, scientists need to restructure their understanding of the material and view it in a new way. This Darwin/Wallace coincidence shows that new analogies or oblique sources clearly help theorists make this 'paradigm shift'. Clearly theorists should actively study fields of work analogous to their own.

Malthus's essay was very famous in Darwin's time, and many naturalists must have read it without making Darwin's and Wallace's discovery. Could some of these also have made Darwin's discovery if they had consciously applied the ideas they found from analogous or oblique sources such as Malthus to their studies? Why not try the conscious use of such 'idea mapping' yourself?

Consider all possibilities (CAP)

Suppose you were asked to design an automatic waterer for indoor plants, so that the owners could water their house plants while they were on holiday. Before considering the details of any design you may consider how the device might be powered. There is a finite number of possibilities: mains electricity, battery, gas, gravity, elastic band, clockwork, petrol, gas, sunlight, capillary action, no power at all ... etc.

In the inspiration phase we leave doors open. Never close them, because you never know where they might lead until you have explored beyond them. Designers Consider All Possibilities (CAP), however unlikely some ideas might appear at first. This ensures you do not pass over a useful solution for no good reason, but there is another, more subtle gain. This is best shown by an example.

When a department store was considering where the pharmaceutical dispensary was to be sited they considered having it on the second floor. This was an outrageous suggestion because it would be so inconvenient for elderly and sick customers. But it had the advantage that the dispensary customers would pass other goods in the store, and so might make an impulse purchase. Eventually the dispensary was positioned on the ground floor, but it was placed next to the escalator, and careful consideration was given to what other wares were placed near the dispensary's waiting area. This increased sales in that area and an advantage of an abandoned solution was preserved.

CAP is for choosing between a relatively small number of possibilities. A musician could CAP in order to decide which bass note best harmonises a short melodic passage. Each note would simply be tried in turn. A dress designer could consider all the possible fixings for a dress: zip, buttons, clasp etc. It is important to expend real effort on each possibility. What are its advantages? What issues does it raise? What factors, positive or negative, does it bring into focus?

Trawling

Consider an interior designer searching through a colour chart or a graphics artist browsing through a collection of business cards before designing one for a client. Or think about an architect on the way to work, looking at bay windows on existing buildings before designing one of his own.

Trawling is a methodical search for ideas or for suggestions which might lead to ideas.

> Henry Moore often roamed the seashore, picking up curious pebbles and shells that fed his current interests, and his work seems to owe something to the weathered shapes of pebbles.

Trawling does not necessarily involve copying. The architect might use the guttering details from one design, the glazing from another and combine all these with original ideas.

Learning without copying

You will learn much more from trawling if you can learn without copying. How is this done?

First, look at the example of good practice and focus on the aspect of the work that pleases you. Ask yourself:

❏ What exactly was done and how?
❏ Why is it successful?

The last question is crucial and should help you to determine the general principle of good practice that you can learn from the work. For example, an artist might like 'the light' in an impressionist painting. They may decide that the tree shadow is where the light is most vividly successful and learn from careful examination that a mottled mix of colours has more vibrancy than a solid slab of the same colour.

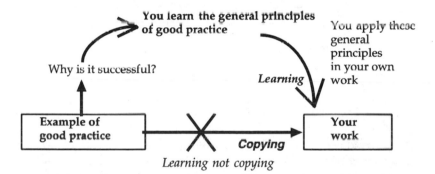

Learning not copying

Once this lesson has been learned there is no limit to how it can be applied without copying. The brush technique does not need to be copied, nor the subject, nor other aspects of the style. Indeed the general principle may be applied without anyone guessing its source. The idea has become integrated into your own approach. This is not copying, but learning and developing through critical observation—something every creative person must learn to do. If you still find yourself copying, go back to your influence and keep asking 'Why does this work?' Keep stepping up until you have a sufficiently general answer. Then try to step down the logical levels again to find out how to apply these ideas in a different way. Moving up and then down logical levels is an ideal way to learn. It is a kind of logical pogo movement allowing you to adapt good practice—the 'logo-pogo'.

Many creative people trawl virtually all the time. Like Henry Moore on the beach they are always on the lookout for ideas—it might be for an unusual colour combination, a clever turn of phrase or an interesting chimney construction. Try to develop this 'magpie mind' yourself.

If all your ideas are self-generated your output will tend to be 'samey'. But trawling forces you into an eclecticism which can often get you out of this rut.

> If you work in a design or problem solving team it often helps to have a mix of people with different experience. This increases the vocabulary of ideas and experience that the team can trawl.

Trawling practice

This activity will develop your trawling technique; consider for a moment where you can trawl for ideas. Depending on the field in which you work you may find some of the following useful:

❑ Journals or books with examples of good practice or advice on technique. (Though you can also learn what not to do from poor work.) Browse through your public library for likely sources.

❑ Consider starting a scrapbook or journal for ideas you come across, adding comments about what you have learned. You could even start your own personal 'how to' guide.

❑ People are often the best sources: for innovation in the business world 'How does so-and-so do it?' is an obvious question, yet it is often not asked. The lift problem could be solved by talking to someone who works in a similar building and discovering how their business copes with the problem.

❏ You should maximise trawling time so, when possible, begin trawling long before you start work.

When trawling you need to be uncritical and open minded, looking for what works rather than condemning what does not. It is often possible to learn from one tiny aspect of a piece of work that is otherwise unsatisfactory. You need to be ready to adapt any idea you find as you may not find it in a perfect state. Allow what you come across to set you thinking, try to remain impressionable and ready to follow a train of thought set off by what you have found.

Brainstorming

Brainstorming is a well-known method of producing a large number of creative ideas for *subsequent* evaluation. It is usually done in groups. The rules are that:

❏ all ideas are welcomed, however offbeat or daft (as wild ideas can often suggest more practical ideas or be tamed to produce useful contributions)
❏ the group aims for quantity not quality
❏ judging ideas is not allowed
❏ ideas are common property, and combining or improving previous ideas is encouraged.

The task should be clearly defined, for example 'How could a retail store increase sales at Christmas?' Ideas are written on a flip chart as they are suggested; this is a full-time activity for one group member. Everyone should be able to see the suggestions: advert in the paper; give the stuff away; Christmas tree outside the shop; give people free coffee; offer a Christmas present ideas service; . . .

If the group flags, give them a one-minute 'incubation' period and then start up again. Once the brainstorming session has dried up, choose the most useful ideas. If there is no consensus this can be done by each person ticking their favourite five or by awarding points, rather like the Eurovision Song Contest. Alternatively ideas can be chosen for satisfying agreed criteria, for example. 'Must be cheap to implement; must not require special training; must not involve extra staff' etc.'.

Now the ideas themselves are brainstormed to decide how they can be implemented in practice:

How would a 'Christmas present ideas service' work?

How could the store go about giving people coffee?

There is a vote for the two daftest or funniest suggestions, for example, 'Give the stuff away'. Now ask, 'Is there any sense at all in this suggestion?' Discussion might then lead to the idea of giving away one free present to anyone spending more than £20.

Evaluation of the ideas is best done on another day. Brainstorming is great fun, but surprisingly, research shows that people can produce almost twice as many effective ideas when working alone.

Backtracking

If one is at a dead end it is often helpful to go back a few paces and take a different route. To take the plant watering example again, if the design team was experiencing difficulty developing a cheap electrical design, they could 'backtrack' and look at a gravity fed design. This may seem like an obvious strategy, but it is often ignored in practice as it is hard to abandon an idea in which there is a large investment of time or emotion—even if it will never work.

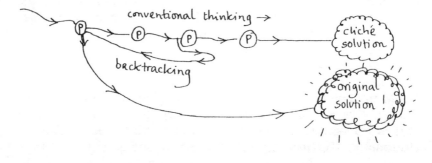

ADVANCED INSPIRATION TOOLS

Advanced improvisation

❏ Imagine that you have within you a separate personality which improvises. This person is childlike and works for fun. You have no real control over this playing child, but watch it as if it were another person as it takes over your hands and eyes. The child's ideas are crazy but provoking, and you laugh at many of them. You have to ask this person if you can use any of his or her ideas.

❏ Similarly you can personalise your internal critic. Say your critic is not wanted and to go away. 'I'm playing. You have no right to be here. Sod off.'

❏ Some painters and writers pass into a reverie, and completely remove conscious control. They close their eyes and look at images from their unconscious or listen to narrative as if it were coming from someone else. They are waiting for direct communication from their unconscious. This takes practice, and the results are rarely coherent, though often provoking. Don't try to manipulate the images or narrative. Just relax and 'listen' for the voice or 'look' for images. This technique will be further considered in Chapter 10 on incubation.

You do not even have to leave your room. Remain sitting at your table and listen. Do not even listen, simply wait. Do not even wait, be still and solitary. The world will freely offer itself to you to be unmasked, it has no choice, it will roll in ecstasy at your feet.

Franz Kafka

Random association

Analogy, oblique sources and trawling all confront you with an unlikely and unfamiliar way of looking at what you are doing. They knock you off the rat track, and from this new position you work back towards your work in progress, usually by association. The hope is that in doing so you will come across a useful idea. If you really appreciate this, then the 'oddball' nature of some inspiration techniques begins to make sense.

Random association also knocks you off the rat track, but uses a different and wilder stimulus. It can dump you anywhere. Random association, like CAP, was pioneered by Edward de Bono. It sounds eccentric, even laughable. But try it seriously for half an hour, and further recommendation will be unnecessary.

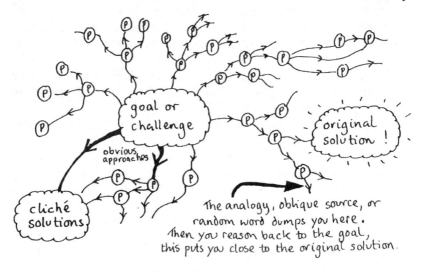

The inspiration rat track

Simple nouns are chosen at random from the dictionary and then word association is used to work towards the desired subject matter. Here is an example of this technique being used by a student who is looking for the subject for her painting entitled 'Human Group' which is to be entered in a competition. The nouns in bold on the left are those generated at random from the dictionary.

recite → poem or reading → group as an audience at a poetry reading
revelation → religious revelation → angel appearing to group of shepherds

glove → hand → handshake → group of people meeting for the first time
glow → fire → group of people round a camp fire.

Random association can be used in any form of creative work, devising the plot for a short story, problem solving, composing ... It is particularly useful for generating fresh approaches. Here I have used random association on the lift problem:
fork → branching into two → could each lift shaft have two lifts in it, one above and one below? This could double the carrying capacity
flow → could peak flow of people to the lift be reduced by staggering working hours and lunchtimes?
fund → could people be required to pay (to charity?) for a badge enabling them to use the lift?
font → font of wisdom → is there some expert on lifts I could consult?

I restricted myself to words beginning with 'f', so imagine how many more ideas I could develop if I used the rest of the alphabet. Mindboggling. I also tried fob, fold and fool, but these suggested nothing to me.

De Bono says that around 40 per cent of words make no useful suggestions, but that you must be really persistent with each word. Don't make the association chains too long, however. Do not link the random word to an existing idea as this defeats the object.

There are other ways of developing the random stimulus. For example, a fabric designer could throw cutouts from magazine pictures on to a white background to look for interesting shapes or colour combinations. Or they could peer at leaves on the floor of a wood!

David Bowie is said to cut out words and phrases that appeal to him from newspapers and magazines, and he then randomly orders them to produce song lyrics or ideas for them. You can use objects you chance upon during the day too; any source will do so long as it is randomly generated.

I always think of myself not so much as a painter but as a medium for accident and chance . . . I don't think I'm gifted. I just think I'm receptive . . . I think that I have this peculiar kind of sensibility as a painter, where things are handed to me and I just use them.

The painter Francis Bacon. Quoted by David Sylvester in
The Brutality of Fact

It is important to realise that the ideas do not come from the random source, but from you. The random stimulus merely knocks you off the rat tracks, you do the rest. Most people are irrationally resistant to this technique. I was at first, but I use it all the time now.

Problems cannot be solved by thinking within the framework within which the problems were created.

Albert Einstein

Provocations

This is another de Bono technique. A provocative statement is made which is clearly ludicrous but would be very convenient or interesting. Rather than rejecting the statement, it is worked on to see if it yields any useful or productive ideas. For example, suppose a designer was working on a design for a flower pot that waters itself while the owner is on holiday:

Po: suppose the plant could water itself. ('Po' stands for provocation)

After a little thought this may lead to the possibility of water transpiring or evaporating from the plant's leaves being put back into its soil. This might lead to the idea of putting a plastic covering over the plant so that water could not escape from the plant and pot. Po is particularly useful in group work. You should have no idea where the po will lead you. You can provoke by exaggerating, by negating an assumption, by wishful thinking and simply by nonsense. Try mining ideas from these:

Po: plants need to swim in water
Po: plants don't dry out.

Po: the moon could do the watering

As ever in creative thinking, you will not get a bite for every line cast.

Record initial thoughts

Scribble maniacally on first getting an idea or brief. Try a wild, wide-ranging exploration before you become aware of how the detail might close options. This is especially helpful before you hear of the expectations of others. Refer back to this later.

Change focus

Difficulties often concentrate our thought on the narrow area where the problem is manifest. Yet the solution may lie elsewhere. For example, when considering the lift problem it is natural to focus on the lifts themselves. But we could change the focus to:

The people who use the lifts → Why do they use them?

The people who do not use the lifts → How do they manage without them?
The stairs → Why are they not used?
etc.

Don't let difficulties direct your focus. If you deliberately develop the habit of changing focus, you will be well rewarded. If you focus on what others ignore, a little creative thought can often produce spectacular and original results.

Before and after

This tool is most useful in overcoming difficulties associated with people's behaviour. Rather than concentrating on the behaviour itself, as nearly everyone does, you change focus to:

Before: *focus on the circumstances that usually precede the difficulty.* Can these circumstances be changed so that the difficulty is not triggered?

After: *focus on the consequences of the behaviour for the person who is behaving inappropriately.*
Can these consequences be changed in some way so that the behaviour is not encouraged?

Here is an example. A teacher expects a verbal apology from any latecomer to his class. One persistent latecomer tends to give comical explanations to raise a laugh from his mates. Rather than telling the student off with ever greater force the teacher could use 'before and after' to change focus, and avoid this difficulty. See if you can do this.

How did they do that?

It can't be done, its impossible! Lack of self-belief can dishearten any inspiration session. One way around this is to imagine yourself in the future, after the work has been successfully completed. Then ask—how did you do that?

Another approach is suggested by a true story of a group who came up with a very radical idea for a bandage manufacturing process. They wanted to take the concept to the company's expert but, as one of them said: 'Norm, like most experts, will just spot why it can't be done'. So they told Norm there was a rumour that the Russians had discovered, and then successfully implemented the idea, and that it worked beautifully. Norm was greatly excited and immediately began speculating how the Russians had done it.

A variant is to suppose you had asked some hero whose work you really admire how they would approach it. You receive a clear, step-by-step account of how to proceed from them. What did they say?

Play

Einstein reported that he often enjoyed a 'vague play' with the concepts he was working with. Play is the natural way to learn, and a joyful and purposeless meddle with ideas can often produce chance combinations of ideas that are productive. To be childlike is not to be childish. Children are astonishingly creative in play and we can learn from them.

Opposites

Try doing the opposite of what is expected. This is particularly useful in artistic creativity. At the very least it gives you the advantage of surprise.

Mind mapping

Mind maps help you to analyse a situation and to develop your understanding of it. This may then help to suggest ideas. There is a mind map which summarises this book at the end of the book.

What happens if none of this works?

At the very least you will have freed up the way you think about your work and discovered what does not work. A failed inspiration session is no indication of waning ability, nor an indication that the task is impossible. You have to sit on some eggs to hatch them—see Chapter 10 on incubation.

IMAGINATION AND THE BRAIN

Research has shown that the two hemispheres of the brain specialise in different tasks; they seem to think in different ways.

The left hemisphere specialises in language, numbers and in that step-by-step, logical thinking we found people using unsuccessfully to solve the candle problem. This hemisphere analyses. It breaks problems or ideas into fragments and focuses on one fragment at a time. This left hemisphere cannot see things as a whole; experiments show that brain-damaged people, able to use only their left hemisphere, cannot even recognise the most familiar face without a laborious checklist: 'Has the face a moustache?' 'Are the eyes green?' The left hemisphere focuses

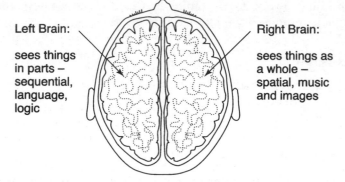

Left Brain:

sees things
in parts –
sequential,
language,
logic

Right Brain:

sees things as
a whole –
spatial, music
and images

The two hemispheres of the brain

on parts of the whole, so it can't see the wood for concentrating on the trees.

The left hemisphere specialises in the rational examination of parts. This is why it is not thought to be a major contributor to the generation of ideas.

The right hemisphere specialises in forms and patterns, spatial manipulation, musical appreciation, images and pictures.

The right hemisphere sees things as a whole. It assimilates all the components of a problem or a situation, whether this is visual or not, into one overall picture. It sees the wood rather than the trees, perceiving ideas in terms of form and structure, rather than in the detail of their parts.

It can focus on similarities. It is good at metaphorical or analogous thinking. It can infer the general pattern from a range of particular examples of a phenomenon, so it specialises in induction or hypothesis making rather than in deductive logic.

Many psychologists believe the right hemisphere to be the seat of intuition and imagination. But how do you tap into it? The answer is by avoiding the exclusive use of rational and analytical thinking, by adopting the right mind-set.

The right hemisphere is not enough however; creative thought requires the full cooperation of both halves of the brain. Inspiration along with incubation are perhaps principally 'right brain' activities, but clarification and evaluation are clearly 'left brain'. There seem to be profound anatomical reasons, as well as emotional and theoretical ones, for turning off rational control while searching for ideas. If you only think logically and analytically, you may be looking for ideas in the wrong half of your brain!

> Dr Roger Sperry was the first to draw attention to this stark difference in cognitive styles between the two hemispheres. He showed that developing the whole brain improved all the functions. So, for example, right brain activities actually improve logical thought. However, the modern school curriculum is thought to spend less than three hours a week on right brain activity. Many great minds developed both sides of the brain. Albert Einstein was a creditable violinist and artist. Mozart adored mathematical puzzles.

THE INSPIRATION MIND-SET

Think of all those ingenious, beautiful and astonishing ideas waiting to be discovered. This is the plain of possibility and it is the aim of the inspiration phase to explore it to the full. To make some of these ideas yours you must not nip into the plain of possibility for ten seconds and then sprint back with the first half-decent idea you find. You must explore it thoroughly for as many ideas and approaches as possible. Do not explore it for perfectly formed ideas either, but for something worth exploring, worth working on.

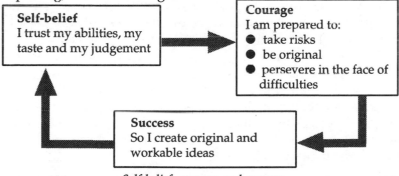

Self-belief, courage and success

Your imagination is a virtually infinite and largely unexplored resource; how effective you are at mining it depends not so much on your imagination, but crucially on your mind-set while exploring it. To discover as many ideas and approaches as possible you need to be deeply engrossed, fearless and free:

Fearless

Bold, risk-taking and even reckless where necessary. Prepared to question assumptions. Unself critical and indifferent to the opinion of others.

It is self-belief which unlocks your creativity. If you believe in yourself (at least temporarily!), you will be more adventurous in your idea generation, and less likely to give up in the face of difficulties. This increased boldness and persistence is likely to improve the quantity and quality of your creative output, which in turn increases your self-belief, so creating what is known as a 'virtuous circle'. The more creative you are, the more creative you become.

There is, of course, a negative version of this cycle. If you begin a task with little self-belief you will be over-cautious and will give up too easily. As a consequence your meagre creative output will be poor in quality, which only serves to confirm your initial lack of self-confidence. This is a 'vicious circle'.

If you have suffered from low self-belief for some time this will have depressed your creative productivity, so your work to date gives an unflattering impression of your true calibre.

It is important to recognise that both the vicious and the virtuous circles are 'self-fulfilling'. Whatever your assumption about your capabilities at the start, your creative work tends to justify it. As a consequence it is possible for talented and capable people to prove to themselves that that they are inadequate or mediocre. Your ability is probably limited more by lack of confidence than by lack of talent.

Positive beliefs are permissions that turn on our capabilities. Beliefs create results. 'Whether you believe you can or you can't do something . . . You're right!'

Joseph O'Connor

Given the importance of this self-belief cycle, you need to think positively and suspend judgement.

❏ Be **receptive**: Adopt a playful curiosity towards unusual ideas, asking what they have to offer, rather than condemning them as impractical.

❏ Be **accepting**: Accept vagueness and incompleteness, don't worry about such practicalities yet. Don't say 'Why?'; say 'Why not?'.

❏ Be **optimistic**: Concentrate on what works in your ideas, not on the questions, problems or paradoxes. Banish scepticism and doubt! These come later.

❏ Be **uncritical**: Don't blame yourself for mistakes or silly ideas. These are a sign of ambition, fearlessness and originality! Only think about it and you will agree! So when you come up with a lousy idea, congratulate yourself. Try to develop a taste for the really awful ones!

This uncritical open-mindedness is fun, but very hard to achieve at first, especially if you have had a run of bad luck. However, research shows that highly creative people are invariably optimistic, at least during this idea generation phase. They tolerate unresolved problems and paradoxes, leaving them for later. If you concentrate on problems, if you are sceptical and questioning, then you will deflate the self-belief and trample over the spontaneity you require for idea generation. Then you will soon run into the mud of your own scepticism and come to a halt. So keep working, keep generating ideas, leave the problems and questions until later, as you are not even at a draft stage yet, nothing is irrevocable and nothing can be spoiled. Remember, this is just exploration.

Alice laughed. 'There's no use trying,' she said 'one can't believe impossible things.'
'I dare say you haven't had much practice' said the Queen.

Lewis Carroll, *Alice Through the Looking Glass*

Don't forget, rationality gets his say, including an absolute veto on any unworkable ideas, in the later phases of the creative process, in evaluation and in clarification. So don't let your self-censor be an overbearing and controlling bully: tell him he has his turn later, and to clear off. Meanwhile, take risks freely, for you are protected by the safety net of these later phases.

Tell him he has his turn later and to clear off

If we had to say what writing is, we would have to define it essentially as an act of courage.

Cynthia Ozick

Many of us, right from school, have lived in fear of ridicule, humiliation and sarcasm. If this fear of criticism is strong it can create a craving for acceptance and approval which overpowers your ability to think independently and creatively. You over-protect your ego by adopting conformist ideas and playing safe. This is hardly an appropriate mind-set for idea generation. You must find the courage to stick your neck out and to shrug off criticism. It is so much easier to remain uncreative and to snipe at the ideas of others, but that will not develop your potential. So where do you get this courage? The answer is partly by coming to trust your own taste.

Trust your own taste

So you have had some good ideas; but you don't trust yourself:

'It was only me that thought them up . . . so they can't be any good can they?'

'All the talented and respected people have a different
approach . . . I must be off beam.'
'They won't like this.'
'I'm not sure I can make this work.'

Everyone has these self-doubts.—Even the most successful?—
Especially the most successful, as they have most to lose and
most to live up to. But you must learn to overcome this self-
doubt and to think positively about what you do, especially in
this inspiration phase. There is plenty of opportunity for criticism in the evaluation phase with its very different mind-set.

How can you get to think more positively? You will find much
more on this in Chapter 9 on evaluation. But here is a crucial
thought experiment for anyone who has difficulty accepting
their own taste, or trusting their own judgement.

Try trusting your taste

This activity will help you trust your own taste. Think of
someone who has criticised your creative output. It might be
your boss, a friend or a judge in a competition. Imagine you are
going to a restaurant with them. Would you let this person
choose your meal from the menu for you? No: and why not?
Because you know what you like, better than they do.

How would you respond if they said, 'I don't like your choice
of soup'?

Imagine you are going to a clothes shop with them. Would
you let them choose your clothes for you? No . . . You know
what you like, better than they do.

And the same goes for your creative output. As there is no
absolute measure of taste, you must learn to trust your own.

*A great deal of contemporary criticism reads to me like a man saying: 'of
course I do not like green cheese: I am very fond of brown sherry.'*
GK Chesterton

Van Gogh sold only one painting in his whole life, and that was
to his brother.

Try trusting your judgement

This activity will help you trust your own judgement. If you are a problem solver, or a decision or policy maker, the issue may be about your judgement rather than your taste, because for you there is often an objective standard, that is: do my ideas work? If your ideas have been fairly tested, then you are lucky and you will know where you stand. Most people have not had their ideas tested, in which case it is your critic's judgement against yours.

Think of one of your critics.

Is his or her judgement infallible? If not, they may be mistaken about your own work.

Is their judgement often poor? If so, you might do better to trust your own judgement rather than theirs, and so ignore their criticism.

Is their judgement nearly always poor? If so, you need only worry when they like what you do!

Here are some activities that help you to trust your own taste, and to have faith in your own ideas and judgement.

Activity

This activity will help you test your censor.

1. Look carefully at someone else's work in your field. Choose work of about your own standard, be this beginner, amateur or professional. Don't choose outstanding work, but a reasonable effort that others have found acceptable.
2. Now examine the work in detail, as if you had just produced it. If you find yourself highly critical, nit-picking, anxious and dismissive, contrast this with your earlier evaluation that the work is generally considered to be acceptable.

Activity

This activity will help you learn to admire your work.

Think of someone who works in your field whose ability you admire. Think of a friend, or failing that, a hero of yours.

Choose some of your own work in progress.

Now imagine that the admired person has produced this work and that you are peeking a look at it in draft form. What do you think of it? You should find yourself making excuses for shortcomings and admiring what you usually take for granted. If the work now seems good to you, then it is good!

Deeply engrossed

Unselfconscious, spontaneous and enjoying the 'here and now'. Joyful, enthusiastic and intensely involved.

❑ You need to be actively digging around for ideas rather than waiting for them to strike you.

❑ You need to be playing around with your ideas (improvisation), not reverently protecting them from alteration.

❑ You need to be open-minded and exploratory rather than close-minded, strategic or tactical.

❑ Try to work quickly. Speed can help prevent self-critical reflection and self-censorship. It also builds enthusiasm.

❑ Try not to invest too much time or effort on any given idea at this stage. Work very roughly—this is not a first draft. Desire for perfection or even neat presentation can make you too cautious when you need to be bold, risk-taking and experimental. You may even just be working in your head at this stage, putting only some ideas down in a more permanent form.

❑ In the field of the arts you are unlikely to produce your best work in a low level of arousal. Many people find they need some intensity, energy or excitement in order to generate their best work. It is not only in performance arts such as music that intense emotional commitment gets results.

This enthusiastic, spontaneous approach generates plenty of energetic effort. It helps ideas flow better and makes you more prolific. Spontaneity helps you to express your individuality, making your work more genuine, truthful and original, and less hampered by unhelpful conventions. Work of a high quality often has an instinctive and unaffected fluency which is not just the product of careful polishing. Next to it, lesser work seems laboured and contrived. Fluency, originality and truthfulness all come from spontaneity.

So loosen up. Give yourself permission to be yourself! Follow the whim, trust your intuition and, oddly enough, don't try too hard. Rather than struggling against things, try flowing with them. Many artists argue that you should surrender the will, that you should not struggle against yourself or the medium, but flow with both. So, at least at times, follow rather than lead; trust rather than try.

> In the inspiration phase, playing safe is very dangerous.
> Although there is plenty of room for crazy ideas and for fantasy, there is no particular merit in craziness, and you need not set out in search of it.
> Many novelists simply watch or listen to their characters and then write it down, many don't know how the story will end until they have written the last chapter.

Aim for a playful immersion at this stage in your work. Be receptive, savouring and enjoying the work, and the experience of generating ideas. This intense engagement can lead to a highly productive self-forgetfulness, a childlike joy where you are totally immersed in the here and now, your whole person blissfully absorbed by the task. You are so engrossed that there is a loss of ego. You are soul surfing. You are exploring and realising what you are capable of, and so becoming yourself.

> *You need only to have seen him at work, painfully tense, his face as if in a prayer, to realise how much spirit went into the task.*
> Rainer Rilke describing Cézanne in a letter to his daughter

> *What's done is done. The joy is in the doing.*
> William Shakespeare, *All's Well That Ends Well*

Even if you do not yet experience this total immersion, do your best to enjoy the inspiration phase, if only because you will then visit it more often, and so get more and better ideas.

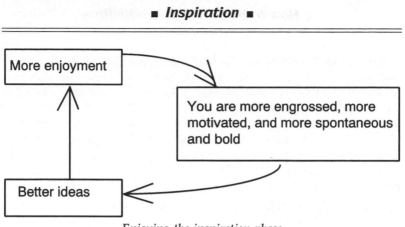

Enjoying the inspiration phase

> In the field of the creative arts this inspiration phase is often associated with deep identification with the subject matter, with empathy and with spirituality.

Free

Uninhibited by notions of what is expected or acceptable. Unrushed, free to explore your own unique individual approach.

Avoid early acceptance

The positive inspiration mind-set must not lead to a premature acceptance of a promising idea. The longer you look, the more ideas you will get and there may be better ideas to come. In the plain of possibilities you must be a tourist—not a commuter! So avoid the common mistake of rushing into a first draft before fully exploring the possibilities.

Remember, the first catch is rarely your biggest. For example, we have had a range of ideas for the 'lift problem', and many people would advocate implementing some of them. But, as you will see, the first-rate ideas are yet to come. Rushing into early closure means implementing third-rate ideas. So try to keep to a playful, ruminating and speculative mind-set, and flirt with many ideas before entering into an engagement with one of them.

'But I can't afford the time! I have to get things done!' But what things do you mean? Third-rate things? Creative people are the growing tip of humanity, they make tomorrow and they can only grow things in the right direction if they are given the time creativity requires. Give yourself time whenever you can and demand it from others.

Avoid early rejection

There should be little or no consideration of practicality, form or quality of ideas, at this stage, and you should not be worried about what is expected or what will be accepted. We will see in Chapter 9 on evaluation that ideas should be judged on their potential to deliver what is genuinely needed. It is too early at this stage to make this judgement, as the eventual solution to the lift problem will show.

> Bernard Berenson defined genius as 'the capacity for productive reaction against one's training'. Eva Hoffmann said, 'It may be freedom rather than necessity that is the mother of invention.'

There is an innate conservatism in us all which tends to make us reject the new and the different. It is as though we have a preconceived view of what 'the answer' should be like. But the better the idea is, the stranger it first appears. So look out for your conservative tendency and challenge it.

> Albert Einstein realised that if an area of science was already well studied, all the obvious solutions to a still existing problem would already have been discovered. An entirely new approach was required: 'If at first the idea is not absurd' he said, 'then there is no hope for it.'

Adopting the inspiration mind-set

How do you approach creative work? It would be most surprising if you always managed to follow the advice above. By
contrast with the inspiration mind-set I have just described,
imagine a typical meeting at a place of work. The boss raises a
problem no one has ever heard of before and demands that you
provide an immediate solution. People are mercilessly critical of
any idea that is not predictable and already perfectly formed,
and you are desperately trying to guess what is acceptable to
the boss rather than wondering what you would do if you had
an entirely free hand. As a consequence, the first apparently
half-decent idea is immediately adopted, only to create another
problem for the next meeting.

If you work somewhere where suggestions are requested well
in advance of a meeting, where even odd proposals are dis-
cussed with an indulgent and playful optimism, and where there
is a reluctance to make the final decision before a full exploration
of all the alternatives, then you are indeed lucky. And you
probably work in a very successful organisation.

If you do your creative work alone, which of the two meetings
I have described best outlines what is going on in your head?
We are often even more intolerant of ourselves than we are of
others.

'Uncreative' people, or organisations, don't give themselves a
chance. By adopting the wrong mind-set they tie their own
shoelaces together. But how can we untie these laces to allow
ourselves to run full tilt into the fulfilment of our capability?
That isn't easy, but the next two activities start the long journey
of improving your mind-set.

Mind-set questionnaire

This activity will check if you use the inspiration mind-set. Think
back to the 'inspiration' phases of your last few creative sessions
and answer the following questions.

Yes!! Yes No No!!

1. Did you trust your own taste or judgement?
2. Did you suspend judgement and remain open-minded?
3. Did you accept ideas that had difficulties?
4. Did you persevere in the face of difficulties?
5. Were you confident and optimistic?
6. Did you take risks?
7. Were you uncritical?
8. Did you ignore what was expected or acceptable to others?
9. Did you avoid early closure?
10. Were you unselfconscious, uninhibited and spontaneous?
11. Did you trust rather than try?
12. Did you work quickly and with enthusiasm?
13. Were you exploring your own unique approach?
14. Did you enjoy it?

SCORING THE QUESTIONNAIRE: Yes!! = 2; Yes = 1; No = 0; No!! = –2. If you left one blank score it as a zero.

Creative people are so self-critical of their approach, that some can score no more than five on this questionnaire. So a low score may simply indicate that you have high expectations of your mind-set! A score over 20 may mean you are too complacent.

Rather than worrying about the total score, look at the questions you did least well on. These suggest areas for improvement and experiment, as outlined below.

Experiment: How to improve your use of the inspiration mind-set

Isolate from the above questionnaire the aspect of your inspiration mind-set that most needs changing. Express this need positively, for example, 'I need to be more spontaneous and more uncritical'. Then try working like this as an experiment, if necessary on work you are not worried about. If all you do is read this book any benefit will be short lived and partial. In order to benefit fully you must experiment with new approaches.

Experiment: Making use of the inspiration tools

Try experimenting in the same way with the inspiration tools mentioned earlier in this chapter. Not all of them will work for you. That's fine. You must find your own way. But beware of rejecting a tool if you have only tried it once or twice, or if you have used it rather half-heartedly

You will probably put up a resistance to tools to begin with. But if you persevere the tools will start to work, releasing ideas that would not otherwise have occurred to you. Of course the ideas are still coming from you, not the tools. The tools just release your imagination.

The 'failed' inspiration session

Everyone occasionally experiences an intensive but barren inspiration session. But, as described in Chapter 10 on incubation, however barren, you have not wasted your time. Your unconscious and your conscious will continue to work if you give yourself time, and you will find a way sooner or later, though you might need to remove a lot of spoil before finding your diamond.

We haven't finished with idea generation yet. The 'clarification' phase described in Chapter 6 can suggest unexpected places to look for ideas, and so will finally solve the lift problem for us. There are some useful tools in Chapter 10 on incubation too.

Here are some solutions to the candle problem, along with

the analogy idea (e.g. 'shelf') that inspired them. If you didn't get most of these ideas you probably didn't use the analogy tool seriously enough. Without the analogy tool few manage more than two of these ideas and most don't get any of them.

Many of the ideas are not good ones—but you wouldn't dream of criticising them would you? This is the inspiration phase! No, you will be looking for ways of making them even better! How this is done is the subject of the perspiration, evaluation and incubation chapters.

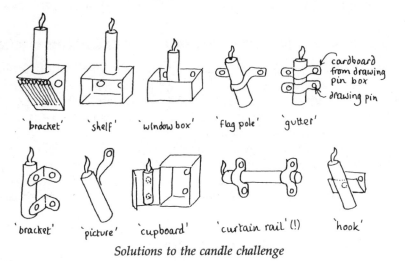

Solutions to the candle challenge

LISTENING TO YOUR EXPERIENCE

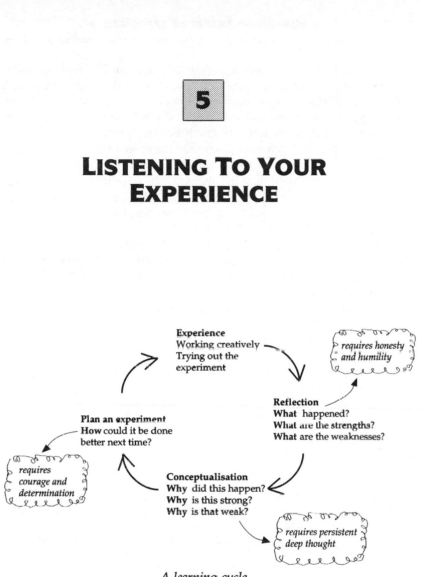

A learning cycle

The cycle above is based on Kolb's reflective learning cycle. It shows that whether we learn from experience or not depends on how we think about that experience afterwards. Look at it carefully before reading on.

We need to ask ourselves, 'What happened?' and give an honest reply! Then we need to ask, 'Why did this happen?', which is often a very difficult question. Then we need the courage to consider how we could do it better next time, and the determination to actually try this experiment out.

Adopting a new approach to your creative work will probably make you awkward and self-conscious at first. This may make you work less effectively to begin with. It is rather like trying to correct a fault with your driving. Adopting a new approach to, say, gear changing, requires unlearning bad habits, doing things in an unfamiliar way and thinking about techniques you normally take for granted. All this will initially decrease your competence. Only after considerable practice will you be able to adopt the improved approach naturally. Not until then will your driving improve.

There were activities involving reflection and experimentation given in the last chapter. Try each of your experiments more than once and accept it if you get worse before you get better. At the end of subsequent chapters, go round this cycle by yourself, reflecting, conceptualising and planning your own experiments or new approaches.

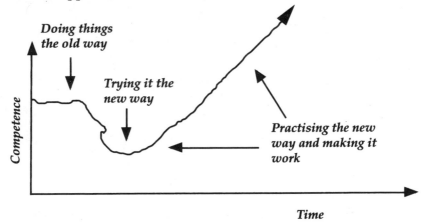

Learning a new approach

CLARIFICATION

Creative work is often a difficult journey, where every footstep is a struggle. It is easy to spend all your time peering at the treacherous ground at your feet, agonising about the next step. But if your eyes never leave your feet, you will not arrive where you intended. The solution of course is to look up from time to time to check you are on course. Even explorers with no pre-planned course need to know where they are and in what direction they are heading.

The main aim of the clarification phase is to discover where you are heading, to find the meaning or purpose of what you are doing. The clarification questions are:

❑ What exactly am I trying to do? What do I want to achieve? What is my key purpose?
❑ What am I trying to say? What do I want to communicate?
❑ What should the finished work be like?
❑ What exactly is the problem I am trying to solve?
❑ What is my key idea here?

In more open-ended work the questions are:

❑ How could I exploit the ideas I have had?
❑ Where could this idea take me—what could I make of it?

And in times of trouble:

❑ What has gone wrong exactly?

It is impossible to appreciate how powerful these questions are until you have tried them. They can remove 'blocks' to progress, revitalise your motivation and help you make difficult decisions. They direct your creative energy with great efficiency, allowing you to achieve more and in less time. They enable you to discover hidden assumptions and ensure that you are solving the 'real' problem. They can also show up weaknesses in apparently good work, allowing you to make improvements where you thought none were possible. They can give your work a sense of focus, that increases its power and effectiveness.

If you are 'blocked', 'lost' or are annoyed by your aimless pottering, then ask yourself the clarification questions. It doesn't matter if you cannot answer them yet, just so long as you know that you cannot answer them! If you keep them in mind, eventually the questions will help clarify your thoughts and intentions, and you will be much clearer about how to proceed.

Many people are surprised to hear that creative work involves answering such tough, logical questions. There is a myth that very creative people have no need for reason and need only follow their mysterious instinctive gift. They might do this sometimes, but not for long without asking 'What am I trying to do here?' Without clarification questions like this, your work too easily descends into meaningless self-indulgence.

Every creative person I have ever talked with is adamant that clarification questions need asking and answering. You might expect this of problem solvers and designers, but painters, poets and actors are all equally adamant. A rock musician, a director of a play or a garden designer might all interrogate an idea that has occurred to them, asking: 'Does it contribute to what I am doing here or does it detract from it?' And they will have the discipline not to adopt an idea which, although superficially attractive, is at odds with their overall purpose. Musicians working on arrangements have an adage: 'When in doubt, leave it out'. Very creative people are often surprisingly disciplined, at least in this respect.

What is not constrained is not creative.

Philip Johnson-Laird

CLARIFICATION IS A PROCESS, NOT AN EVENT

Only occasionally is the creative act a dutiful working out of a preformulated idea. It is often an ongoing search for meaning or purpose in the work. Such uncertainty is not a sign of weakness. R Arnheim studied how Picasso approached his masterpiece 'Guernica' which portrayed Picasso's horror at a war atrocity. It had many preparatory sketches, and underwent many revisions. Arnheim wrote: 'Picasso did not simply deposit in Guernica what he had thought about the world; rather did he further his understanding of the world through the making of Guernica.' Creative people of all abilities report a similar learning process, a slow crystallisation of the meaning and purpose of their ideas as they work on them.

Clarification of wholes and parts

A writer needs to ask the clarifying question, 'What exactly am I trying to say or achieve here?', about a novel in progress or indeed about their whole writing career. But they can also ask the question about a chapter, a paragraph, a sentence or even just a single word. These parts also need clarification, but so do other parts of the whole, such as the characters, themes, writing style, dialogue, plot, use of humour and so on. The clarification questions need asking about each of these. Each part has its purpose, has a contribution to the whole and has relations to other parts, and these need clarifying.

Parts I can clarify

Every kind of creative work has its parts and its whole. Painters talk of colour, texture, tone (light and shade), line and composition. What are the 'parts' in your line of work?

Clarification is not easy. When clarifying parts you are so focused on the detail, that you can easily lose sight of 'the big picture'. You need to be aware of what contribution the part makes to the whole and to keep this in mind while working.

Unless this is achieved the parts will never harmonise into a coherent whole. There is nothing mystical about this; it is a matter of clarity of purpose.

A piece of work of the highest standard, in any medium, often has an overarching character, concept or purpose. When every part of the work helps to achieve this purpose then the work has a sense of unity and coherence. Artists and designers call this overarching vision or logic: 'form', 'structure' or 'concept'. In contrast poor work often seems 'confused' and 'arbitrary', and lacks a sense of purpose or direction. Ideas have been chosen because they appealed at the time, not because they fulfilled the greater purpose.

OPEN AND CLOSED CLARIFICATION

In closed work you have an objective or problem in sight:

'How can I package this product?'
'I need a new approach to painting sky.'
'Staff turnover is too fast to get continuity on long contracts.'

Open work has no definite end point:

'I like this shape, what could I do with it?'
'What sort of personality should I convey for this character?'
'How could I improve the efficiency of my business?'

Sometimes the main purpose of the intended work is clear from the start. For example, a designer may be given a detailed brief by their client. More usually they need to interrogate and negotiate to discover the client's needs. But once the brief is decided, designers are taught to refer constantly to this brief as they work. This is surprisingly difficult to do.

Sometimes, however, you may start work with only a hunch that there is 'something there'. This is absolutely legitimate. You want to explore some idea that takes your fancy with only the vaguest notion of where it will take you. Some novelists, for example, work in a very open way, not knowing in advance how their story will proceed.

In open-ended work, clarification is an ongoing process best explored with the open questions listed at the beginning of this chapter. You may only achieve a full sense of purpose and meaning at the very end of the work. Then you may need to go back over the work with this clarified purpose or meaning in mind to remove ambiguities. The mistake is not to try to clarify. If you are not clear what your work is about, then you cannot expect to communicate this to others. However it must be admitted that the very greatest artists seem able to break this rule.

> The strategy of starting off before you know where you are going is sometimes called 'Fire . . . Ready . . . Aim.'

Clarification questions

Try asking yourself the clarification questions every five minutes or so during your next creative session. Ask it about parts as well as the whole. Don't worry if you can't answer the questions, just go on working with the questions in mind. As your purpose becomes clearer, you will be able to work much more decisively, and with fewer blocks.

If you attend meetings try asking clarification questions such as: 'What exactly are we trying to achieve with this proposal?' There will often be a stunned silence. But when the answer is found to your question the way forward may be blindingly obvious.

> Sometimes, clarification goals need to be prioritised, or compromised: 'Is it going to be cheap or high quality?' Then you will need to make a choice between the goals or strike a compromise between them.

THE THOUGHT–ACTION CONTINUUM

This section of the book is fairly tough. I have simplified it as much as possible, but it is still tough. This is not because it is difficult, but because it is odd. The ways of thinking it describes seem puzzling and foreign to most people. You may need to read the next pages two or three times. You will also need to practise the techniques described for some time before you become fluent with them. Just reading this section is unlikely to do anything for you; the techniques described need to become a habit of mind.

But it will all be worth it. This section describes the Houdini logic that creative people use to escape the rat tracks of conventional thinking.

To illustrate the use of the thought–action continuum I am going to consider an example of problem solving, but the methods are identical, and equally powerful in artistic creativity, the strategies being particularly useful for overcoming creative blocks or challenges. Indeed, what follows is relevant whenever you act for a purpose.

On page 30 we considered 'the lift problem'. A managing director had received repeated complaints from his employees that they often had to wait several minutes for the lift. During Chapter 4 on inspiration we used tools such as analogy to suggest solutions for this problem. But we have not solved it yet.

If you have a problem, or indeed any situation where action is being contemplated to meet a purpose, it often helps to think of it in terms of the thought–action continuum. See page 83. Then it helps if you can escape from it.

You will usually start in the middle of the continuum, with an objective or need. This is what you are trying to do. Clarification is in part the process of deciding what purpose this need serves and whether it is a real need. Let's take for example the objective: 'To reduce the waiting time for lifts'. Once the objective has been stated clearly like this, we can step up or step down the thought–action continuum in the following way.

To *step up* the continuum ask 'WHY?', meaning: *'For what purpose?'* or *'What causes this need?'* In stepping up you are asking for the reasons for this need.

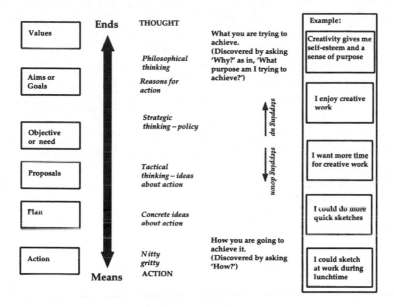

The thought–action continuum

To *step down* the continuum ask 'HOW?', meaning: *'How can I do it'* or *'How can I meet this need?'* You are asking for actions that would meet your needs.

We have seen a similar stepping process being used to move up and down a hierarchy of categories in Chapter 4 on inspiration. This is a similar but not identical process.

Let us deal with the relatively simple and very familiar process of stepping down first.

Stepping Down

Here is an example of stepping down:

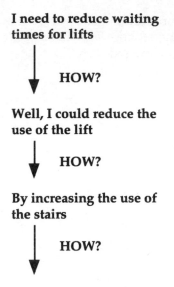

I need to reduce waiting
times for lifts

HOW?

Well, I could reduce the
use of the lift

HOW?

By increasing the use of
the stairs

HOW?

When you are stepping in any direction it is crucial to be able to focus exclusively on the statement you are stepping from, ignoring the other statements. This takes practice.

'HOW' is a very useful and pragmatic word. It craves detail and makes us think our plans out. But note:

❑ It is often necessary to ask 'HOW?' repeatedly. Most people only ask it once or twice. They accept a surprising level of vagueness in their plans.
❑ Inspiration techniques can give you many alternative answers to each HOW question. (We found many alternatives using the analogy tool in Chapter 4 on inspiration.)

Stepping up

Stepping up clarifies the 'real' purpose you are trying to serve or the real cause for your action. A world of ingenious ideas opens up when you are fully aware of these real reasons for needs, or your real problems or challenges. Most people don't step up to these, and deal only with the needs or problems as they first occur to them or as they were first presented. To find 'real' needs or reasons keep asking yourself 'WHY?', meaning: 'What causes this need?' or 'For what purpose?' Again it is often necessary to do this repeatedly.

Start with a clear statement of your need:
    'I need to reduce the waiting time for lifts.'
    WHY?
    'Because at present the lifts are inadequate.'

Most people would accept this reasonable statement and stop stepping up. Don't! Keep asking the WHY question to get as many different reasons as you can. Allow reasons to overlap, be messy and open-minded, leave time for pondering and incubation. Later you might neaten up your ideas and put them on a step-up diagram like the one shown below. Read the diagram from the bottom up.

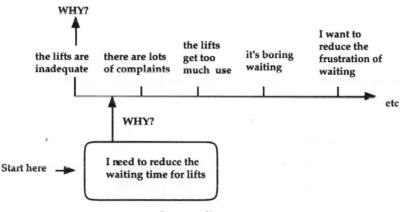

Step-up diagram

I bet you think this looks unpromising, but it will solve the lift problem for us! Step up again from each of the reasons at the top of the diagram. For example, '**Why** are the lifts inadequate?' Because the waiting time is too long? No, this is a circular argument which lands you back where you started. You have stepped *down* rather than stepped up.

'WHY?' questions usually have lots of possible answers, so we need to choose the non circular ones. So let's try again: **'Why are the lifts inadequate?'** Because they are old-fashioned, because they are slow etc. And why are are they old-fashioned? Because they are in an old-fashioned building! This may seem obvious, but it leads to the suggestion that the business should move to newer premises. This is not a bad idea, which would have been lost if you were sucked into that earlier circular argument.

Stepping up gives you 'real' reasons and reasons can suggest solutions. One way of obtaining solutions from reasons is to ask:

'SO . . .?' after each reason.

'SO . . .?' steps down the thought–action continuum to the action which the reason suggests, rather like 'How?' does. Here are some examples:

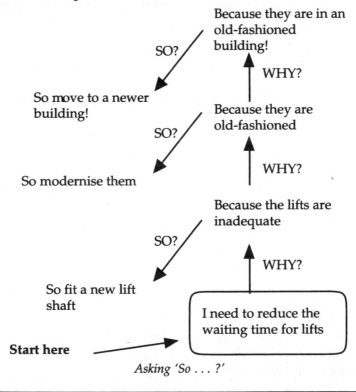

Asking 'So . . . ?'

Look at the 'So . . .?' figure again. Use 'WHY?' to step up as far as you can, and use 'SO . . ?' to suggest more solutions. Focus particularly on reasons which one might have influence over. This should suggest ideas, but avoid 'early closure'! The brilliant solutions come to those who don't stop at the good ones!

Ask an impertinent question and you are on the way to the pertinent answer.

J Bronowski, scientist

Sidestepping

We have stepped down and we have stepped up, now it is time to step sideways. This is lateral thinking. In order to illustrate this I am going to use a simplified version of a stepping-up diagram. Look at it carefully, reading it by starting at the bottom of the diagram. By the way, can you add a further step-up without being circular?

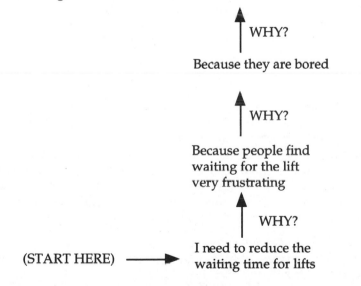

Simple step-up diagram

Now we will try sidestepping from each statement on the step-up diagram. There are three sidestepping words or questions (these will become clearer when you see the examples later).

UNLESS ...! as in 'unless I ...'. This asks for a circumstance where the statement would no longer hold. It looks for a way of avoiding the statement.

OR ...! as in 'or I could ...' 'or we could change the need to ...'. This asks for an alternative to the statement or the circumstances it describes. (It helps to use EITHER with 'OR ...?' as the examples later will show.)

NO! ... as in 'No! that's not true!' (denial) or 'No! the opposite is true!' (reversal). This challenges the statement on the step-up diagram.

These are the most powerful problem solving words on the planet. They often enable you to escape apparently impossible situations in a single bound. They should be written in huge letters over the desk of every person involved in creative work. They are the key to challenging assumptions, and to finding false dichotomies, so they force you into lateral thinking.

You can use 'UNLESS! ...', 'OR! ...' and 'NO! ...' to sidestep from any statement, but sidestepping from the statements on a step-up diagram is particularly productive.

First I will show you some sidesteps from the statement—'There are lots of complaints'—on an earlier step-up diagram. Once you have seen these examples I will give you some sidestepping to do and in doing so you will solve the lift problem.

To sidestep simply read the statement you are sidestepping from, followed by the sidestepping word. Then wait to see if an idea suggests itself. Try to wait for some considerable time with the sidestepping word 'hanging in the air'. Try it now.

'There are lots of complaints':
UNLESS? ... you forbid complaints, explaining there is nothing you can do.
EITHER (there are lots of complaints): OR! ... people are complaining when they shouldn't be. (Is the lift problem being overstated? Are people using it to get at management?)

NO! . . . there aren't that many complaints, perhaps we should talk to the people who don't complain and see how they cope? . . . Perhaps we should do a survey?

Statements like 'there are lots of complaints' or 'we need to reduce waiting time' are expressed as emphatic certainties. The real world is much fuzzier than these apparent certainties suppose, so it is important to challenge our reasoning at every stage. Sidestepping looks for exceptions, hidden assumptions and downright errors in our thinking.

Sidestepping is not easy, but you get better with practice. Remember to focus exclusively on the statement you are stepping from, and to think hard and long. Incubation can help.

The ideas you produce will tend to repeat themselves or repeat ideas you obtained using 'SO? . . . '. Sometimes the sidestepping words will suggest no ideas at all. That is to be expected, as creative thinking isn't that easy! But on other occasions you will get really useful ideas

Sidestepping practice

Look at the simple step-up diagram on page 85 and try sidestepping from all the reasons at the top of the diagram. Do this before reading on. You will need pencil and paper.

Here are a few of my sidesteps for the diagram on page 82. Remember that *every* sidestep word should be preceded with the statement you are stepping *from* (shown in quotes). You should focus hard on this statement, not on the preceding sidestep. I have missed out the more unproductive sidesteps!

'*I want to reduce the frustration of waiting*'.
NO! it's a nice rest to wait.
UNLESS! . . . you make waiting interesting by providing some sort of entertainment.

'*I need to reduce the waiting time for lifts*':
UNLESS . . . I can get people to accept the waiting time in some way.
EITHER '*I need to reduce the waiting time for lifts*'

OR . . . reduce the number of people using them
OR . . . encourage alternative ways for people to get together
OR . . . put people who communicate with each other a lot on the same floor . . . OR . . . etc.
NO! the waiting time is perfectly acceptable, stop fussing!
NO! let's make use of the time for corporate communications. What about a noticeboard?

'The lifts are inadequate:'
UNLESS . . . I can speed them up . . .
EITHER *'The lifts are inadequate'* . . .
OR! . . . too many people are using them.
NO! slow lifts are fine, they encourage informal communication.

'The lifts get too much use:'
UNLESS! . . . you encourage people to use the stairs, the telephone and the post

'It's boring waiting:'
UNLESS! . . . you make it interesting.

Now these are really productive ideas! (Note that each sidestep comes from the original statement in italics, not from the previous sidestep.)

You will remember that the managing director asked for quotes to fit a new lift shaft and got quotes for millions of pounds. But the contract was eventually awarded to an engineer who submitted a £60,000 interior design. When asked for a quote for a new lift shaft he was the only one who stepped up by asking 'Why'. He was told about the complaints. The work time lost by a two-minute wait for the lift was negligible, so he realised that the 'real' problem was not the lifts, but the complaints.

His solution was to make the area where people waited attractive, comfortable and interesting. There was a seating area with newspapers, magazines, fish tanks and mirrors. This solution still works well to this day.

Most people don't bother to step up, let alone step sideways. They accept the need as soon as it is stated and then ask 'How can I meet it?' When you first read about the lift problem in the inspiration chapter I bet you accepted the need to reduce the waiting time of the lifts without question! If you did step up and sideways you are one in a million. But you can become one in a million by simply remembering to use these stepping tools. Then you will often open up a hugely abundant treasure trove of original ideas. But like all creative tools, it will not work every time.

I bet you forgot to use 'SO? . . .' on the above step-up diagram! Try it now to see if it suggests ideas.

Denial and Reversal: 'Reframing'

Reframing takes place when you use denial or reversal with NO! . . . Many of our ideas and practices are a matter of convention or habit. Denial or reversal challenges these and can produce very original outcomes.

Buddy Holly needed to wear glasses but he wanted to be a pop musician. Most people in his position would have limited the damage by unobtrusive, frameless glasses, or not worn any at all and stumbled about blindly on stage. Instead he decided to deny the assumption that glasses were 'square' or unattractive. And he wasn't half-hearted, but wore very heavy, black-framed glasses.

There is nothing good or bad, but thinking makes it so.

William Shakespeare

Another aesthetic denial was made by the architects of the Pompidou Centre in Paris, Richard Rogers and Renzo Piano. For centuries 'services' such as water pipes and ventilation ducts had been hidden in the structure of buildings. Instead the ducts and lifts were brought to the outside of the building, and painted to make them a feature. Note that denials or reversals are nearly always emphatic.

The denial strategy is very useful if you need to make a virtue of a necessity.

The above examples are of an evaluation being denied, but a need can be denied too, or a reason. Denials are most successful when the need or reason is a matter of convention and no real purpose is served by it. Stepping up will of course discover this lack of purpose. Why are electrical sockets placed so you have to bend down to make use of them? Why do windows stop at hip height when they could go down to the ground?

Denial practice

Examine a typical piece of work in your field; an architect might choose a three-bedroom house.

Look at each basic feature of the work (walls, doors etc) and challenge, deny or reverse each one.

Step up to find the purpose and then deny this: 'What is a door for? To keep the heat in. NO! We don't need internal doors with central heating.'

Step down to their typical characteristics and deny these: 'Doors are 2 m by 1 m. NO! Why so small? If door-holes were bigger they would create a sense of space. Why rectangular? An arch would be stronger and more attractive.'

Step left to find their conventional evaluation (this is their assumed advantages and disadvantages) and deny or reverse these:

'Sound proofing? NO! It's an *advantage* to be able to hear from room to room. Someone cooking in the kitchen would enjoy talking to people in the sitting room, or listening to the hifi or television.'

Focus on the *disadvantages* of customary practice, and the *advantages* of any alternative you have thought of. Does this suggest how to evolve any impractical ideas that denial has given you?

How far do I step up?

So you should step up before you step down, but how far? If in doubt, step up again as one more why question won't waste time. Don't be in a rush to the concrete level or you may find yourself working on the wrong problem. Many people fail to step up because they regard their purposes or any other causes for their action as obvious and irrefutable. Sometimes they are, but it is surprising how often they are not.

When you get to the top of the thought–action continuum you will find self-evident value statements such as 'because people prefer to be free' or 'because people do not like being bored', or 'because you should not waste money'. Values like these are the ultimate reasons for all actions.

If you find a statement such as 'because my boss or client has told me to', don't stop stepping up. *Why* has your boss or client told you to? If you understand the 'real' reason, you are more likely to meet the 'real' needs, and may meet them in a novel or creative way. The engineer who solved the lift problem was the only one who asked his potential client *why* the new lift shaft was needed.

Stepping up is not natural for most people, but it must become a habit for you if you are determined to be a really creative thinker. Really able people invariably think deeply about what they are doing and *why*. But like every creative tool it will not bear fruit every time.

Step up practice

This activity will give you some step-up practice. Step-up to help solve this problem.

You are an assistant manager of a hotel and the manager wants the florists' bill to be halved from the present £700 per week. Flowers are important as they give your hotel a fresh and attractive atmosphere, so you have them in every room, as well as in the foyer and restaurant. Plastic and other synthetic flowers are ruled out entirely, as they are too 'downmarket'. Step up to find some novel solutions to this problem.

Stepping up for artists

Many 'artistic' people would regard stepping up as cold, logical thinking suitable for engineers, but entirely alien to their intuitive and emotional approach. The notion that creativity never involves logical thinking is a debilitating myth.

Great artists agonise throughout their working life over the ultimate purpose and meaning of their work. They are forever asking why? Indeed, the greater the artist, the more they tend to question accepted ideas with this question. It was only when, in the middle of the nineteenth century, that painters started to question the assumption that the ultimate aim of painting was to represent reality as literally as possible, that the impressionist movement began. Artistic movements such as impressionism, cubism, surrealism or dadaism in painting, or, say, satire and magical realism in literature, are formed around the questioning of assumptions about the ultimate purpose of their art.

I see but one rule: to be clear.

Stendhal

'It seems to me it's a painter's duty to try to put an idea into his work . . .'
Van Gogh in a letter to his brother

Similarly, movements in design have been formed around shared ideas expressed in maxims such as 'form follows function' or 'a building is a machine for living'. (These examples describe the functionalist aesthetic which abhors decoration, but every creative movement has such assumptions and maxims.) Many artistic movements have gone so far as to publish manifestos outlining their values and aims. For example, the 1910 Manifesto of the Futurist Movement of painters and poets begins by saying that there is a growing need for truth in art, and that all things move and run and change rapidly, and this universal dynamism is what the artist should strive to represent. There follows a series of numbered statements outlining their aims in more detail.

Those who regard art as essentially decorative have been mystified by such movements and their declarations. Artists, whose sole aim is to have their work liked, have been similarly puzzled. But great artists almost invariably spend a lifetime thinking hard about what they are trying to achieve in their work, though they can change their mind often. Picasso went through a number of radically different 'periods', realist, cubist etc, each characterised by a different conception of the meaning and purpose of his work.

Once this meaning is clear it drives the work. The theatre director Peter Hall tells of the time when actors thought their only purpose was to present a fully rounded character. Then Brecht 'pointed out that every actor has to serve the action of the play, but until the actor understands what the true action of the play is, what its true purpose is . . . he cannot possibly know what he is serving.' The parts must serve the whole in the same way, whatever the medium. But this requires a very clear notion of what the 'true purpose' is of what you are making.

Your own manifesto

Most people find the process of clarifying what they are trying to achieve an enormously difficult, but fascinating, and ultimately extremely helpful activity. Try writing your own manifesto. Take your time and don't be afraid to change your mind.

As well as writing a manifesto for your work as a whole, you can try to write one for a piece of work in particular. Such a succinct statement of intent is a natural outcome of the clarification questions.

Elephant traps in the arts

There is a remarkable consensus about the nature of high quality art. But those who write about the subject are often connoisseurs or great artists themselves, so they set a very high standard. They warn against the following.

Attention Seeking

Novelty, surprise or shock have no artistic value in themselves, neither have what Tolstoy called the low animal feelings of disgust or lust. To be affected by something is not to have had an artistic experience.

Neither is art mere decoration or entertainment. Its aim is not simply to please or to disturb, but to say something unique and insightful and to express strong feelings about high values. A painter might express feelings of reverence about nature, a musican might express joy and a poet or dramatist feelings concerning justice. Trivia doesn't seem to get a look in I'm afraid!

The search for novelty and originality is an artificial need which barely conceals banality and absence of temperament.

Cézanne (whose paintings were shockingly original in their time)

Indulging in private rhetoric

The aim of art is to communicate. The poem is not what the poet means, or even what the poet writes, but what the reader understands. A poet with something important to express should not, indeed will not, bury their insight beneath obscure writing.

Imitation art

Tolstoy argued that poor artists often imitate the work of others, rather than exploring their own sensibilities. Even great artists are influenced by others, but this is largely unconscious. If their true goal is the authentic expression of their own deepest feelings they will eventually find their own way and their own voice.

Painting is a blind man's profession. He never paints what he sees, but what he feels.

Picasso

Seeing in categories instead of observing first hand

Stereotyped characters and cliché-ridden prose show a writer is seeing things in broad categories instead of focusing on the unique and the individual. Artists have an innocent eye; they see things directly, as if for the first time. They are not swayed by the perceptions of others, or by habitual or careless observation, instead they look very deeply, for themselves. This fresh perception, focused on what is unique and individual in their subject matter, is the basis of originality.

Consoling rather than being truthful

To take extreme cases, Barbara Cartland's novels have been criticised for portraying an unrealistic view of romance, and Rambo films an unrealistic portrayal of conflict. Some commentators regard such lack of truthfulness, not as playful escapism, but as a great danger. They argue that the combined effect of large quantities of such bad art perverts people's taste for real art, and perverts their understanding of love and conflict in their own lives. Also, violent films for example may condone and therefore excuse immoral behaviour such as revenge or hatred. At some deep level art is important, and must be honest and truthful.

History tells lies with the truth, but fiction tells the truth with lies.

You should instead aim to express and vividly communicate strong feelings about what is of transcendent importance to you. The subject matter is only the vehicle for this expression; it is not sufficient in itself. In addition you should see your subject matter in a new and revealing way, and you should convey a unique personal insight which increases our appreciation and understanding of our world. This is a hugely demanding brief, which even the greatest fall short of often. I pass it on to inspire not to dispirit!

When they start on a new piece, artists often begin with an initial conception—a personal vision of how the finished work will be. This is strongly felt, but often very vague. This becomes the vision which drives their work forward.

PROCESS CONTROL

There is a tendency for people to stay stuck at the same level on the thought-action continuum, especially when working in a rush. Pragmatists get stuck at the action level, managers get stuck at the need level and perhaps the next level down, while philosophers and academics stick at the value or aim level. Very few people are able to think right from the top to the very bottom. But if you are involved in creative work this is precisely what you must do. Even when immersed in detail, you need to have in mind your ultimate purpose, the ultimate meaning of what you are doing. It is because many creative people do not know what their real aims are, that they fail to achieve them.

The same goes for many problem solvers. Yet to solve a problem you must continually step up to clarify exactly what you want to achieve and must repeatedly step down to work out how this might be done. But we live in a culture where action is prized above thought, so many of us end up doing the wrong thing, even if we do it very well.

The clarification phase has two main aims. One is to clarify what you are trying to achieve. The other is to decide which of the icedip phases you should be using at any given time. This latter 'process management' is very important. There is for example, little point in implementing an idea with a perspiration phase until you have first evaluated the potential of your idea against your clarified intentions.

The decision making compass

The decision making compass is a tool to help you decide which icedip phase to use. It includes the (vertical) thought-action continuum and the sidestepping 'alternatives' direction examined earlier in this chapter. But it adds to these a fourth thinking direction: evaluation. Evaluation is the icedip phase concerned with gauging the potential or the strength of a creative idea, or of your work in progress. The compass below shows all four productive thinking directions available to you.

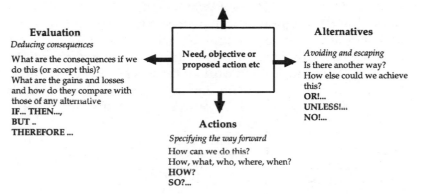

Reasons

*Trying to discover the main purpose
or cause for action*
For what purpose? For what cause?
WHY?

Evaluation

Deducing consequences

What are the consequences if we
do this (or accept this)?
What are the gains and losses
and how do they compare with
those of any alternative
**IF... THEN...,
BUT ..
THEREFORE ...**

Need, objective or
proposed action etc

Alternatives

Avoiding and escaping

Is there another way?
How else could we achieve
this?
**OR!...
UNLESS!...
NO!...**

Actions

Specifying the way forward

How can we do this?
How, what, who, where, when?
**HOW?
SO?...**

The decision making compass

At any given time you can think in the following ways:

❑ **Upwards:** For purposes or causes for action. You can clarify your purpose by asking 'What am I trying to achieve here?'
❑ **Downwards:** For actions. You can try to determine a possible action by asking 'How could I achieve this purpose?' This is the most common thinking direction, the 'What should I do?' direction.
❑ **Sidestep (right):** For escape or alternatives. Stepping right involves looking for alternatives using OR! . . .; finding exceptions using UNLESS! . . .; and trying outright denial or reversal with NO! . . . You can sidestep right from a need, a purpose, an action or an evaluation, indeed you can step right from almost any meaningful statement.
❑ **Evaluate (left):** to look for the consequences of ideas or actions, and so help to decide between them. There is more detail on this thinking direction in Chapter 9 on evaluation.

To move in any direction you will need to facilitate your thinking by seeking relevant information. How many people use the lift in a day? What is the power of the motor? Could it be replaced?

But if you have all the relevant information, then these are the only productive thinking directions.

In practice a surprising amount of our thinking does not go in any of these directions, neither does it facilitate the decisions by searching for information. We are not thinking productively at all, but following an unexamined habit or floundering about aimlessly with difficulties. These are familiar experiences to anyone involved in creative work or those who attend meetings. The cure for either habit or floundering is to decide which direction you need to think in, or to use an incubation phase.

The decision making compass diagram above shows a need in the centre. This is the easiest way to use the compass. However, after a bit of practice you can start with almost anything in the centre. You could begin with a difficulty, a reason, a suggested action or an evaluation. After stepping up, down, right or left from this, you can then step in any of these directions again and so on.

How creative action is avoided

When faced with a difficulty, people commonly avoid thinking in *any* of the four productive thinking directions by adopting one of these attitudes:

❏ **Endure it:** 'That sort of difficulty is inevitable.' This is a self-fulfilling prophesy. If you always do what you've always done, you'll always get what you've always got. But what would happen if you did something different?

❏ **Blame yourself:** 'I'm hopeless! I'll never be able to sort this out.' This is another self-fulfilling attitude. If a strategy doesn't work, then don't blame yourself, don't even blame the strategy, as it might have worked in different circumstances. Simply change the unproductive strategy.

❏ **Blame others:** 'Its John's fault, why should I do anything?' You may be able to change the unsatisfactory situation yourself even though you are not to blame for it. Indeed those who are to blame are the ones least likely to see the difficul-

ties for what they are. You may need to treat John with some
sensitivity though!

❑ **Ignore it:** 'Problem, what problem?' Creative people act for
a purpose; they like to take ownership of the situations they
can see ways to improve, whoever is to blame and whoever
is responsible.

Creative blocks

If you are blocked, or making slow progress, clarify your use of
the creative process by asking yourself these 'process' questions:

❑ What icedip phase am I using? Is it the right one? Or, if you
prefer . . .
❑ What direction do I need to think in: up, down, right or left?
❑ What mind-set am I using? Is it the right one?

Often you will find you are using the wrong strategy, or the
wrong mind set, or both! Creative blocks are only rarely due to
lack of talent or bad luck. Usually they are due to poor management of the creative process. Suppose, for example, you find
yourself aimlessly dreaming up alternative ideas from which
you find it difficult to choose. Novelists often have this difficulty.
Asking the process questions should lead you to realise that you
need to use the clarification and evaluation phases, not the
inspiration phase.

Alternatively you might be staring at a blank sheet of paper
fearful of making a mark. Asking the process questions will then
reveal that you are adopting the wrong mind-set. You need to
adopt the inspiration mind-set and experiment in a fearless and
blame-free manner.

If, however, you are staring at a blank sheet of paper thinking
about what you are trying to achieve you are certainly not
blocked, simply taking aim before you fire.

Thinking direction questionnaire

What is your natural thinking direction or decision making
style? Answer this questionnaire to find out.

Think about your approach to creative work when answering the following questions by choosing YES!!, YES, NO or NO!! Be honest, this is not a time for false modesty. Only you will see the results of the questionnaire after all. Don't agonise; if in doubt follow your gut feelings.

                                        No!! No   Yes Yes!!

J. I carefully balance the pros and cons of different courses of action

J. When I get a good idea I look for possible difficulties or for methods of improving it

J. I look for strengths or weaknesses in almost everything I do

J. I think that on the whole I have sound judgement or taste about my work

J. I am often critical but give credit where it's due

S. I stop and think from time to time while I work

S. I often ask myself what I am trying to achieve

S. I enjoy thinking theoretically and read about work in my domain

S. When I see something that I admire, I often ask how the effect was achieved and why it works

S. I usually have a clear sense of purpose while I work, and if not I am certainly looking for one!

A. I enjoy my creative work, I like actually getting down to it

A. I am keen to see results

A. I like to roll my sleeves up and get down to the nitty-gritty

A. I am frustrated if there is no action

A. In the end it's what you produce that counts

I. Much of my work is innovative, original or can be quite clever

I. I enjoy puzzling out alternative courses of action

I. I think most people of my standard working in my field work in a rather conventional or predictable manner

I. I enjoy challenging assumptions

I. On the whole I can think for myself. I don't need people to tell me how to work all the time

SCORING: YES!! = 2   YES = 1   NO = 0   NO!! = -1

Pencil your score for each question into the score column of the questionnaire.

There are five questions for each of the categories J, I, S and A. Give yourself a separate score for each category. There is a maximum of ten marks for each category.

The actual score you achieve is not important as some people are much harder on themselves than others. Indeed, very creative people are often extremely self-critical. However, the relative scores of the categories will give you an indication of where your strengths and weaknesses lie. What counts is which of your scores are highest and lowest. Most people find they are relatively weak on the strategist and innovator categories. Weak categories show where concerted effort to improve is most likely to be rewarded.

J is for Judge (evaluating by leftward thinking)

If this is your highest score you are critically aware of most of what you do and probably have reasonable judgement. You are very aware of the likely consequences of action and important detail does not usually escape you.

If your score is very high, beware of over-caution. You might be overcritical and perfectionist, to the point of inhibiting your Activist score. There should be a balance between appreciation and constructive criticism of what you do. Destructive criticism is counter-productive, unless you can take it in a genuinely good-humoured way.

If this is your lowest score you may be overconfident and too intuitive. You could probably improve your work a good deal if you were more judgemental about draft work. Read Chapter 9 on evaluation very carefully and do all the activities more than once.

S is for Strategist (finding reasons by upward thinking)

If this is your highest score you are unusual and you have a clear sense of purpose in almost everything you do. You are able to see the big picture without getting lost in the detail.

If your score is very high, beware the head in the clouds syndrome, that is ignoring practical constraints and important detail, or failing to take action.

If this is your lowest score you risk doing the wrong thing, though perhaps doing it very well! Your work would be more focused and well directed if you paid more attention to the clarification process. Make lots of use of the clarification questions at the start of this chapter and remember to step up more frequently.

A is for Activist (specifying actions by downward thinking)

If this is your highest score you are active and enthusiastic, probably with a good fund of self-confidence (even if it doesn't feel like that all the time). You are probably prepared to experiment and have plenty of commitment. However, you may be just a victim of downsizing.

If your score is very high there is considerable danger that you will rush into action before:

❑ exploring the problem fully (Have you fitted any good lift shafts recently?)
❑ planning properly—to fail to plan is to plan to fail.

You may also fixate on tactical objectives (means) and so lose sight of what you are really trying to achieve by these objectives (ends).

The more difficulty you experience, and the more over-worked you are, the more likely this is to be a problem. This is the wasp at the window syndrome; if the wasp can't get through the window it just tries harder, instead of looking for another means to the same end.

If this is your lowest score you lack the ability to apply yourself, but why? You may be too self-critical and cautious to get the best out of your talents. If so, don't be afraid of producing poor work, it is the only route to better work and it is the way you learn. Stop blaming yourself for anything less than perfection, loosen up and try to enjoy your work more. Reread the inspiration mind-set every day for a week! Pay careful attention to Chapter 11 on finding the creative drive.

I is for Innovator (looking for alternatives by sideways thinking)

If this is your highest score you are a very rare bird, inventive and original.

If your score is very high beware of being over-optimistic or impractical. You are probably also prone to the 'reinventing the wheel', and the 'not invented here' syndromes.

If this is your lowest score you are either too modest or you are rushing into action without examining alternative possibilities. The latter is a very common fault and perhaps everyone has it to some degree. So look for alternatives as described above with OR? . . . UNLESS! . . . and NO! . . . Also, try the logo pogo described earlier in this chapter. Give yourself more time before acting, and ignore what others think, trusting your own taste as explained in Chapter 4 on inspiration.

Questionnaire Summary

This is not a scientifically produced questionnaire, but I hope it will help you to decide on your weakest thinking direction. Ideally you should be able to think in any of the four possible directions with equal ease and should always choose the most appropriate direction for the circumstances. In practice we all tend to have preferences, usually due to habit, personality, external pressure or to a mistaken view of the nature of creative thinking. Your preference for a given thinking direction is not a fixed matter of personality. Indeed, it can depend on context. You may be an activist in your personal work, but a judge when you collaborate.

As with a set of golf clubs, you need to choose the club most appropriate to the situation. There is no point using your putter when the hole is 300 m away, however good your putting! You must use the process questions as your 'caddy' to assess the situation and decide which club to use. It is difficult to become better than your weakest thinking direction. However, once you are aware of your weakest thinking direction, you can set about strengthening it by:

❑ using your weak thinking direction whenever it is needed
❑ improving your skills in that direction.

Don't expect quick improvements though, as we saw in 'Learning from experiments' at the end of Chapter 4 on inspiration, real improvement takes time.

A group involved in creative work should ideally have at least one person fluent in each of the four thinking directions. You may need to appoint, say, a strategist if the group is deficient in that area, with a brief to ask the clarification or stepping up questions from time to time. The most common deficiency is the innovator; this role is unpopular as, in challenging the group's assumptions, they can be seen as frustrating trouble-makers. Consequently, many of us voluntarily weed out our innovatory tendencies.

CLARIFICATION TOOLS

We have seen some clarification tools already, in particular the decision making compass, reframing and the manifesto. Here are some others to try.

Asking the clarification questions

If there is one idea I want you to get from this chapter it is that you should ask yourself the clarification questions frequently, both before and during work.

Look through the questions at the beginning of this chapter and choose those appropriate to your work. If you abbreviate any questions to 'Why?', remember that this is only a rough translation of the key clarifying question which is 'What purpose am I trying to serve here?'

A minimum set for a writer might be something like:

- ❏ What am I trying to say?   (for closed work)
- ❏ How could I exploit this idea?   (for open work)
- ❏ What has gone wrong exactly?   (for problems!)
- ❏ What icedip phase am I using?   (to clarify how you are using the creative process as you work)

- ❏ What mind-set am I using?

If you answer these questions mentally, be sure to give full answers. You could try writing your answers down or talking them over with a colleague or friend.

Walking the dog

Clarification can take place at any time. Gains are particularly noticeable if you think about what you are doing fairly soon after stopping work on it. Try clarifying somewhere where you cannot pick up your tools and work—in the bath or when walking the dog.

The best time for planning a book is while you're doing the dishes.

Agatha Christie

Tolerance of ambiguity

Ready, fire, aim.

It is very dangerous to be too methodical in creative work. Do not clarify too early. It is often necessary to explore possibilities before you can know what your aims might be. While exploring you will find that some ideas are unresolved or ambiguous. Some ideas may even clash.

So what? Cultivate an amused indifference to this confusion and keep working on your ideas despite these difficulties. But don't ignore the difficulties; be clear where you are unclear. If you allow yourself time to ruminate on the unresolved and antagonistic ideas, then in time they will synthesise and evolve into a coherent whole. We are such rational creatures that a lack of clarity, once uncovered, simply itches to be resolved. Your subconscious will sort this out for you if you are reasonably clear where the lack of clarity lies and if you give yourself a chance with some periods of incubation.

The best problem definition comes after you have found the solution.

Researchers have found that tolerance of ambiguity is a universal characteristic of creative people. They never rush to evaluation. They are happy to live with paradoxes and the unresolved clashes of half-formed ideas. The tidy approach, which is to use logic to eliminate and to chop away at ideas, can bar you from opportunities if used too soon.

Research

Creativity requires more than ideas, especially for designers and problem solvers. You need knowledge, skills and experience if your ideas are to be sound, and implemented successfully. Of course creative work itself is one of the most absorbing ways of achieving this expertise.

Creative people are not always good at research—dreaming up ideas is more fun than information retrieval or practising skills! So they often reinvent wheels or adopt impractical approaches.

❑ Have you researched the areas you need to understand?
❑ Have you got all the information you need?

❑ Have you talked to the people who will be involved with the implementation of your ideas?
❑ Have you listened!?
❑ Are you getting unbiased information?

If you don't want to 'catch' other people's prejudices and assumptions, note down some ideas of your own before the research phase.

While researching, two common mistakes are:

❑ arrogant indifference or ignoring the viewpoint of others, and
❑ blind acceptance, where you accept as immutable fact your own or someone else's opinion.

You need to listen to other people's ideas with real care, using the uncritical inspiration mind-set. You must accept conflicting information with an open-minded tolerance, at least initially. Later you can be ready to challenge accepted practice, accepted evaluations and accepted 'necessities'.

Analysis

You can analyse a situation by using 'what why when where how and who'

❑ What are we going to do?
❑ Why are we going to do it?
❑ When are we going to do it?
❑ Where will it be done?
❑ How will it be done?
❑ Who is going to do it?

This six question checklist will bring to mind most of the important points you must consider.

Brief

To clarify what you hope to achieve write yourself a 'brief', perhaps in the form of a checklist, which describes your intentions succinctly.

State your intentions positively rather than negatively: 'I don't want it to look like Monet on a bad day' is not very helpful. 'I'm aiming for simplicity, with huge patches of strong greens in the foreground, and plenty of tonal contrast' is more like it. The brief may arise from your answers to the clarification questions.

To write your brief before you start work would be very logical. But you might not be very logical and prefer to develop the brief as you work. Whatever you do, refer to the brief often, and don't be afraid to revise it.

The planning cycle

Managers, teachers, directors, indeed planners of all kinds, make use of a cycle similar to the one shown below. The precise terminology varies between professions, but the meanings remain much the same. The cycle can help you take an overview of how you work, and help in the choice of the appropriate icedip phase. It is a process control tool that can be used for the whole or a part of your work.

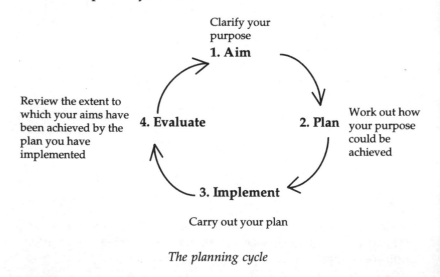

The planning cycle

It is important to realize that this is an improvement cycle and you may go round it many times in producing one piece of work. The first three stages descend down the thought–action continuum from aim (thought) to implementation (action). Here are the icedip phases usually associated with each stage in the planning cycle:

1. **Aim**: Clarification.
2. **Plan**: Inspiration followed by evaluation.
3. **Implementation**: Alternate phases of perspiration and evaluation.
4. **Evaluation**: This is obviously the evaluation icedip phase (the process explained in Chapter 9 on evaluation). Be careful to evaluate the extent to which you have achieved your aim, not just whether you are impressed by what you have done.

If you go round the cycle a second time avoid the well-established error of skipping straight from evaluation to implementation, missing out 'aim' and 'plan'. You should consider whether you want to change your aim in the light of experience.

Some work is more amenable to revision than others of course. A jazz musician would not be able to stop the band and go back to improve his solo. But he might work out how to improve it for the next time he plays it.

The first letters of Aim Plan Implement and Evaluate spell A PIE, which may help you remember the cycle. If you were to make a pie you would go round this cycle, if only intuitively.

Mind mapping

You can explore the territory appropriate to your work with a mind map. Start with a central image or word, and order your thoughts by radiating them out from this, printing key words on the lines or in boxes. Show relative importance by the size of your writing or images, and by the thickness of your lines. It doesn't matter if you can't draw, but try to make it neat and attractive if you can—use of colour helps. You will need to produce a draft before you are able to produce a neat version.

Mind maps help you to clarify, order and summarise your thoughts. See the mind map on the last page which summarises the ideas in this book.

ADVANCED CLARIFICATION TOOLS

Neural networking

You can show your reasoning on a diagram similar to those shown on pages 85 and 86 of this chapter. Such diagrams often get very complex, so again you will need at least one draft before any neat version. Start with your need in a box in the centre of the page. Then use the four thinking directions to produce a record of your reasoning. Write 'Why?', 'Unless!' etc on the lines connecting the statements. From any statement on the diagram you can step up, down, right or left.

Leave apparent 'dead ends' in your network, as this allows incubation to take place. So does putting a rightward arrow on a statement with an OR! . . . arrow leading to a blank space. A glance at such a neural network shows whether you are thinking in all four directions. The tool is demanding, but productive, and is most useful for complex, or over-familiar problems.

Logo pogo

Expect to fall off this particular bicycle a few times before you get the hang of riding it. It is an advanced technique. The logo pogo is a logical jump which enables you to leap over obstructions. First you step up by asking 'Why? . . . What is my purpose here?' Then you ask 'Is there any other way in which I could achieve this purpose?' This allows you to step down to specify an alternative action which would achieve the real purpose.

For big problems you may need to step sideways before stepping down.

In retrospect we can see that the lift problem was solved by a logo pogo:

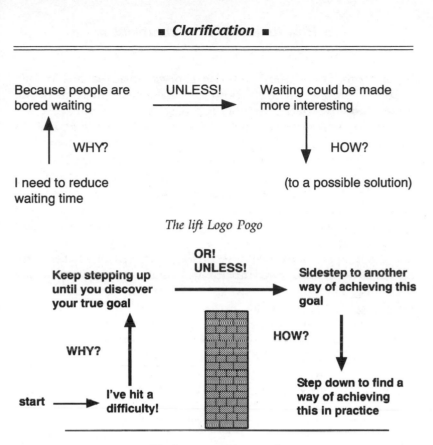

The lift Logo Pogo

The logo pogo in general

The intrinsic and extrinsic 'Why'

This technique can be quite revelatory, transforming difficulties into opportunities. But it takes careful thought. Practise stepping up in the ordinary way first.

There are two, very different reasons for acting. One is because the situation is controlling you. The other is because *you* want to control the situation. If **external** factors are making you act then your motivation is **extrinsic**. If you are acting for your own, personal **internal** reasons, then motivation is **intrinsic**. Consider, for example, the reasons you might give for decorating your living room. There might be intrinsic or extrinsic reasons for this action. There are probably both, but the ones you concentrate on will greatly affect how you approach the problem.

Extrinsic reasons might be: There are cracks in the plaster. Jo says the paint looks shabby. It hasn't been done for years etc. Extrinsic reasons are **external** to yourself; they are the constraints, necessities or expectations of others, which require you to act. Notice that all the extrinsic reasons above are statements of fact, and are mainly negative. The extrinsic 'why' asks: 'What fact causes your need?' The assumption is that you are controlled by the situation.

But action is not exclusively caused by inconvenient facts! As all creative people know intuitively, there are intrinsic reasons for acting. The intrinsic 'why' asks: 'What purpose am I serving here?' and 'Why do I value this need or action?'

Answers to this 'intrinsic why' question will be in the form of personal values rather than facts. The same question, 'Why do I need to decorate the living room?', is now asking for the feelings or values satisfied by the need. This often requires more thought. The answers might be: I appreciate living in a fresh and well-cared for environment. It would be fun if the room were less predictable and had brighter colours. I want to come down in the morning and feel that I am glad to live here. Intrinsic reasons express your values, and your real purposes, so they are usually very positive. You are reaching out for gains that you can make in the future instead of reacting to circumstances created in the past. You are controlling the situation instead of the situation controlling you.

Unfortunately there is a universal tendency, especially when under pressure, to concentrate exclusively on the extrinsic 'why'. But then you are only fending off fate and fulfilling other people's agendas; you are not taking control of the situation to fulfil your own.

In most situations both intrinsic and extrinsic goals can be pursued at the same time. You can respond to external necessities, but at the same time look for the opportunities to pursue your own agenda and do what you think is important. But intrinsic reasons, being forward looking, positive and creative, are much more productive and motivating.

If you are working in a new media or in difficult circumstances, then the extrinsic, 'crisis management' approach is inevitable. If you are a writer, the plot corners you in a situation you didn't expect or desire, and you wrestle with the consequences. If you are in a new business, then circumstances dictate and you obey. Your real needs, values and purposes never get to the top of your in-tray. When a painter first uses watercolour, the paints do what they want to do, not what she tries to make them do, and all of a sudden she is struggling against the medium, trying to contain earlier mistakes, rather than realise opportunities or aspirations.

But eventually, when experience gives you control over the medium you must see yourself as an agent of change and make the world respond to your vision (instead of the other way round). You must begin to hear the 'why' question in the intrinsic sense; you must begin to set yourself intrinsic challenges, goals or objectives. Taking initiative and thinking for yourself in order to please your boss or your teacher is a step in the right direction, but is not enough. You must set your own goals. This is explored more in Chapter 11 on finding the creative drive.

Reasonable men adapt themselves to the world.
Unreasonable men adapt the world to themselves.
That's why all progress depends on unreasonable men
George Bernard Shaw

Do you prefer to think in terms of objectives rather than reasons for action? If so, you can have extrinsic and intrinsic objectives in exactly the same way as extrinsic and intrinsic reasons for action. Extrinsic objectives express necessities and constraints, while intrinsic objectives describe where you want to go despite these constraints. You must have both intrinsic and extrinsic objectives, or you will lose sight of your real purpose, and so fail to realise your hopes.

In old age Matisse lost the ability to hold a paint brush. You might have expected him to despair. But instead he made collages with coloured paper and scissors! The resulting vibrant canvases are the equal of any of his paintings. Triumphing over adverse extrinsic circumstances, by focusing on ultimate intrinsic purposes is characteristic of creative people. Beethoven's triumph over deafness is another example.

Cause-and-effect . . . Purpose-and-action

Few people realize that the word 'why' has two meanings in the dictionary. It means 'for what purpose' (intrinsic) and it means 'for what cause' (extrinsic). If you keep asking the extrinsic why you will step up a cause–effect continuum. Stepping up with the intrinsic why produces a chain of purposes, ending in values. It steps up the purpose–action continuum. So the thought–action continuum is really split into two like this:

Cause   **Purpose**

Extrinsic reasons
Reactive, factual; and negative and backward looking. Focused on necessities.

Why?   Why?

I need to decorate the living room

Intrinsic reasons
Proactive, positive, realising your own vision of the future.

You are on a purpose–action continuum.

You are on a cause–effect continuum.

Effect   **Action**

You are controlled.

You are in control.

Splitting the thought–action continuum

Therapists researching methods to improve the lives of unhappy people asked their clients to take at least some control over their lives by doing a little of what **they** wanted, for their **own** reasons. Even when doing what they had to, they were encouraged to look for ways of doing it their way. This strategy was found to greatly improve their happiness.

THE CLARIFICATION MIND-SET

As with the inspiration phase, you have little hope of clarifying effectively unless you adopt the appropriate mind-set. In order to clarify your purposes (and your management of the icedip phases etc) you need to be *strategic, unhurried* and *impertinent*.

Strategic

We have seen in this chapter that you need to examine your purposes carefully if you are to achieve them. This is not commonly understood. Most people confuse action with progress and clarification is trampled in the rush.

You need to ask the clarification questions about the whole and about the smallest parts. You need to interrogate yourself. What am I trying to achieve here? Where could I take this idea? The answers to such questions are emphatically not obvious. The great geniuses in every medium agonised over them for a lifetime. Amateurs pass over such questions at their peril. Lift your eyes to the horizon—are you heading where you want to go?

You need to be able to step back from your work from time to time, and to look at it in a clear-eyed, logical, analytical way. But you don't need to be bright to clarify. Nobel prizewinners show roughly the same distribution of IQ scores as their fellow students at university. As in other spheres of human endeavour, it's not how big it is, it's the way you use it.

> *Above a surprisingly low level, there is little or no relationship between IQ and achievement in any sphere of adult endeavour yet studied.*
> Professor Liam Hudson, professor of psychology

Unhurried

We have seen that the rush to action makes you think 'down-wards' on the decision making compass, but that you need to think upwards and sideways too. Few people do this. It takes an unhurried mind-set to step back from a piece of work and ask, what am I trying to do here exactly? The activist in us gets impatient. It screams 'Get on with it!' (meaning, do the wrong thing very quickly). Think of the activist part of your nature as a labourer with lots of energy and no brains. Practise telling him to shut up.

Clarification may only take about 5 per cent of the time you give to creative work. However, it saves very much more time than it takes. It ensures that activity is in the right direction, it helps you decide quickly between alternative ideas and it unblocks you when you are stuck. In any case one can often clarify 'off task' and so very little working time is needed. Remember the cliché, more haste—less speed.

Impertinent

You must continually question accepted practice, refusing to accept the views of others (including those of critics, your client and those in authority), unless they stand up to your scrutiny. You must reject even your own expectations. You must be deter-mined to think things out from scratch, for yourself. Independence of mind is a universal characteristic of creative people. It is crucial that real purposes are justified to your own satisfaction.

If you work with others this requires considerable personal skills. Suppose you are an architect. In walks a potential client:

> 'We need an extension on our house. I've a . . .'
> 'What for?'
> 'What do you mean what for? Because it's not big enough.'
> 'No. I don't accept that. You could be using the space inefficiently.'
> 'Look I need another 40 m².'
> 'Unless you can achieve the same purpose with less.'

You wouldn't last long in an architect's office if you treated clients like that! But a good architect does go through these same thought processes—only more politely. (Can you see one step up and two sidesteps in the above conversation?)

Lateral thinking requires the use of NO!, UNLESS! and OR! Stepping up requires WHY? or WHAT FOR? These are very impertinent questions. If you work with others you will need to use tact. You may even need to be tactful with yourself!

It's not easy being strategic, unhurried and impertinent. People have been trying to train you to be the opposite for decades. Teachers and bosses want you to be unquestioning, compulsively active, and respecting of convention and the expectations of others. But this is the mind-set that leads to the frenetic fitting of lift shafts.

It is a common observation that creative people are often disrespectful of authority, unconventional and politically radical. That is because they are strategic and impertinent enough to think things out for themselves. They are independent thinkers.

You must learn to join them; it's an exciting journey.

7

DISTILLATION

So you have generated a pile of ideas—which of these should you choose to work on? You might think that selecting ideas is reasonably straightforward, but it's not. It's often the process that sorts the innovators from the hacks. The main problem is the huge temptation to go for ideas which are:

- ❏ similar to ideas which have worked in the past
- ❏ relatively free of problems or errors
- ❏ the most fully worked out.

This play safe strategy systematically rejects all of your original ideas and most of your best ones. Why? The answer is because it chooses ideas on the basis of nearly irrelevant criteria. You should be looking for the idea which most effectively achieves your purpose, not unoriginal ideas that can soon be implemented. There is something depressingly perverse about passing over promising ideas in favour of the predictable and third rate. Yet this happens all the time. It is important to realise that creative people do not necessarily get better ideas than other people. They just have the ability to spot the better ideas and, most particularly, the courage to work on them.

So how should you make your choice? The key questions when evaluating ideas are not whether an idea seems superficially attractive, but 'Where will this idea take me?' and 'Is that where I want to go?' You must focus on promise and purpose. If you have already clarified then this will help enormously. If not, in choosing between your ideas you should focus on what you hope to achieve by them, and so bring about some clarification.

Most people ignore the strategic questions above and ask instead, 'Can I make this idea work?' This question should come third or you will let workable ideas take you where you don't want to go. In any case you should not answer this third question without an exploratory perspiration phase, however short. How can you know if an idea will work until you have given it a fair hearing? And, remember, it's not the ideas you are judging, it's where the ideas can take you. It's the finished work that counts.

Original and promising ideas are often raw and a bit frightening. That's why most people reject them. I'm afraid you can't expect original ideas to have unoriginal difficulties. They often have very odd difficulties indeed. But trust yourself. Suppose you could deal with these frightening and unusual difficulties? Suppose you could remove these barbs, defuse the bombs and walk round the land mines? You would then be left with an original idea without the deficiencies. Now that's worth working for.

It is worth noting in passing that, outside the chemistry laboratory, few people have died meddling with an original idea. Ideas are fairly benign. They look terrifying, but they can be efficiently disarmed by simply placing them in a wastepaper basket. Never reject an idea on the ground of a difficulty or problem; instead turn the difficulty into a need and then meet the need, as explained later.

So ignore the negative—look only for the positive, for the interesting, for the original, for the promise in the idea. Give yourself some credit for being able to sort out those glaring deficiencies. It is much easier to remove the deficiencies from a promising idea than it is to put promise into a dull idea with no deficiencies.

You must be brave, in the sense of having the courage to trust your own judgement, and your ability to implement your ideas. But do not be foolhardy enough to attempt ideas you do not have the skill to implement. It is a difficult balance to strike, but try to work within your capabilities, without underestimating them. A simple idea effectively implemented is infinitely more powerful than a difficult one botched.

You will get better at choosing ideas with practice; you will develop a personal aesthetic or style and a clarified idea of what you are trying to achieve in your work. In the mean time you will tend to pass over workable ideas and take on ones so riddled with difficulties that even an expert could not make them work. You can only learn the hard way, but we will see later how to make this learning curve as steep as possible.

Evaluating ideas from the inspiration phase protects us from the disasters that would occur if we implemented all our ideas. This makes us feel safer in the inspiration phase when we are 'taking risks' with odd ideas.

If, after using the inspiration tools, you do not have any ground-breaking ideas then choose one that is good enough and work on it as hard as you can. A painter friend told me, 'I'm a great believer in "good enough": out of satisfactory work can come much better ideas'.

> ... *there are no disasters attributable to creative thinking. When disasters do occur they are attributable to the poor assessment of creative possibilities.*
>
> Edward de Bono

As later chapters will make clear highly creative people follow their passions. They abandon themselves to their curiosity or enthusiasm and play with risky ideas for the sheer joy of it. Lesser talents would abandon these same ideas for fear of failure, but great talents enjoy the playful immersion so much, that an unproductive outcome does not concern them greatly Especially if you work in the arts, try to cultivate this playful unselfconscious absorption. Don't be afraid to work on ideas with more interest than promise.

> *I never made a painting as a work of art. It's all research.*
>
> Picasso

DISTILLATION TOOLS
The distillation questions

The main criteria should be fitness for purpose. Keep asking: 'Where will this idea take me?' and 'Is that where I want to go?' If the answers are encouraging do not condemn the idea as unworkable until you have tried it out.

If you cannot answer the first question, try a 'low investment' perspiration phase as described in the previous chapter or parallel working as described below. If you cannot answer the second question, try a clarification phase. Once you have clarified what exactly you hope to achieve with your proposals then the distillation process often becomes very simple. Also, examining ideas which appeal to you, can make your preferred purpose clearer. Distillation and clarification can be mutually supporting phases.

Checklist of criteria

When assessing ideas it helps to have criteria. These can be general or specific.

There is remarkable agreement among creative people in very different fields on their general criteria for a good idea. Here are some that you may like to choose from.

Ideas should be:

simple, elegant, clear, concise, bold, original, beautiful, honest, authentic, fit for their purpose, and there should be a harmony between the parts and the whole.

If you can achieve these your work will have other qualities. Clarity and simplicity give power and immediacy. Fitness for purpose gives effectiveness and so on. You might like to compile your own list of attributes.

Creativity has been compared to the process of evolution by researchers into creativity such as D N Perkins. Interestingly, biologists notice that in the course of evolution designs are selected which show qualities such as concise simplicity, elegance, economy, power and originality—the very character-istics often prized by designers.

Turn weaknesses into needs

You must outline the disadvantages, difficulties or indeed impossibilities associated with your interesting or original idea. But never reject the ideas on the basis of these weaknesses as most people do. Instead, turn the weaknesses into needs. For example, suppose a director suggests very low lighting during the witches' scene in Macbeth: 'We can't drop the lighting—the witches' faces would not be visible.'

Turn this weakness into a need: 'If we dropped the lighting we would *need a way of making the witches' faces visible.*'

An inspiration phase should throw up some ideas. They could carry lanterns, there could be a light in the cauldron . . .

Similarly, 'We can't accept that proposal, Smith would object', becomes, 'If we accepted that proposal we would *need a way of making it acceptable to Smith.*'

Every 'weakness' can be expressed as a need and only some needs will be impossible to meet. Finding ways to meet such needs takes time, but original and promising ideas are worth it. Good ideas are very commonly condemned too early.

Creativity in groups

When groups are involved in creative work there is a notorious tendency to reject an idea outright because of a single weakness. This is especially true where there is conflict or competition between decision makers. Groups should agree to express 'weaknesses' only as needs. This requires practice and considerable restraint, and group training is often needed to agree and then establish the approach. However, this greatly improves the emotional climate and the morale of the group, as well as enormously increasing its creativity.

A similar approach is to sidestep weaknesses using OR!, UNLESS! and NO! as described in Chapter 6 on clarification:

'UNLESS we brought the witches up to the footlights, then we could see them.'
'NO! . . . we don't need to see the witches' faces. It would be more dramatic without.'

'UNLESS Smith got something out of it.'
'OR we could persuade Smith's line manager to overrule Smith's objections.'

While some weaknesses can be dealt with, some cannot be side-stepped, denied, reversed or turned into a need. They are genuine disadvantages. Which is which? You will not discover this quickly. You will need to look hard at them over a period of time. A period of incubation is helpful.

Parallel development

Why choose between ideas at all? You could work on two or three ideas and then choose later. Some ideas are attractive precisely because you can see where they would take you. They are predictable. But don't ignore the underdeveloped and unpredictable ideas which could lead anywhere. Only by exploring these will you discover their potential. The most common error at this stage in the creative process is to condemn ideas without exploring them. So why not work very roughly on two or three?

That one's the tallest!

Help!

If you are working with others, or if others will be affected by your work, shouldn't you consider their opinion even at this early stage? There are often several 'stake holders' to consult and you may learn a great deal from a discussion with them. If they are consulted now they will probably have an increased commitment to the final work. They will add useful suggestions and point out errors or omissions.

Is there someone whose judgement you respect, off whom you could bounce your ideas? Be careful of your purpose in doing this. Are you asking for advice or are you abdicating responsibility for making your own judgement?

Amalgamation

Can you combine ideas and/or their benefits? It is surprising how often amalgamation is overlooked. You may be able to combine the benefits of a number of ideas into one different idea.

Logo pogo

This technique is particularly effective when used on attractive but unworkable ideas. Even if the deficiencies are fatal, a pogo can enable you to run off with the promise in an idea, leaving the deficiencies behind. We have already seen the logo pogo being used to learn from an exemplar and to overcome apparent impossibilities (see pages 49 and 113). Here it does both at the same time.

Before you begin, make sure the idea really is unworkable. Can you turn the disadvantages into needs, deny, reverse or sidestep them? If this doesn't work, try a pogo:

First step up: 'What is the real purpose or value of this idea?' You may need to step up more than once until you fully answer this question.

Then step down with: 'How else could I get this?' (Alternatively you can sidestep before stepping down.)

Let's go back to our witches for an example. Suppose the director decides not to drop the lighting because of the visibility problem. Don't just abandon the idea as most people would, but pogo out of it as described above. Try this yourself before reading on.

Step up: Why do you want to drop the lighting? Because it creates an eerie, frightening atmosphere, and a contrast with the previous and later scenes.

Step down: How else could I get this? An inspiration phase could uncover many possibilities: mist; odd coloured lights; creepy creatures like bats or spiders; eerie sound effects; eerie music etc. This seems obvious in hindsight as creative solutions often do. But it is important to recognise that most people fixate on 'lighting' and 'visibility' and never extricate themselves from this initial problem, like a wasp trying to fly through a closed window instead of the nearby open one.

SWOT analysis

If we must rigorously compare major ideas or proposals, then we should first list the strengths and weaknesses of each proposal, and then try to sidestep each weakness or turn the weakness into a need.

Then we should look to the future and list the opportunities and threats we can see for the proposal there. Again threats should be sidestepped or turned into needs whenever that is possible. Then, for each proposal we have the Strengths, Weaknesses, Opportunities and Threats (hence SWOT). You might have some needs too. A rigorous comparison can then be made between the alternatives.

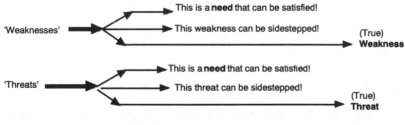

Comparing the alternatives

People are notoriously unsystematic in evaluating ideas. There seems to be a natural tendency to rush the choice and to be bounced into acceptance or rejections by just one strength or one weakness of one idea or proposal. It's easy to see why when you try to be rigorous with a SWOT analysis, the process of making an informed decision is very arduous and time consuming. Most people hate being this rigorous.

If you consider rejecting all the ideas and abandoning a project as a result, then this abandonment is a hidden idea or proposal in itself. I say hidden because it invariably escapes full evaluation. For example, an executive may reject every proposal for training staff because they are all too costly. But what is the cost of **not** training the staff? This may be greater still. The executive needs to include this 'hidden' non-training option in the SWOT analysis.

Buridan's ass

You have two ideas which are identical in terms of advantages, needs, disadvantages and opportunities. Which one do you choose? Buridan's ass is said to have been placed equidistant from two equally attractive bales of hay and, unable to choose which one to eat, starved itself to death.

If you can't decide between ideas, then it doesn't matter which one you choose. If, however, it is difficult to know in advance which idea will yield the best result, then you could consider parallel development as described above.

THE DISTILLATION MIND-SET

In order to choose which ideas from the inspiration phase to work on, you need to be *positive, strategic* and *intrepid*.

Positive

You look for the opportunities and the potential in your ideas, trusting yourself to be able to tackle the difficulties.

Strategic

Rather than choosing familiar and easily implemented ideas, you must know exactly where you want to go and choose ideas because they take you there.

Intrepid

You must aspire to be an·audacious free spirit, and an adventurous explorer of your own passions, obsessions and ideas. And your guide in this fascinating and uncharted land, your sole map and compass, is your own judgement. You do not refer to the judgement of others, to habit, to fashion or even to the expectation of success. You are driven by a fearless and playful curiosity.

Diamonds are not very beautiful in the raw state. It is the skill of the diamond cutter that reveals the beauty of the diamond. So the value of ideas is only revealed by those who set out to make the ideas work.

Edward de Bono

8

PERSPIRATION

So you have used the inspiration phase to obtain ideas, the clarification phase to decide where you want to go and the distillation phase to decide which idea was likely to get you there. Now you have sharpened your pencils, rolled up your sleeves and cleared some space on your desk. How do you feel?

Some people can't wait to get started, but most people's problem at this stage is lack of self-belief. As explained on page 62, whether you believe you can create valuable work or not—you are right. To make an idea work you need persistence in the face of the inevitable difficulties and perseverance to bring it to completion. None of this is possible without self-belief.

Increasing self-belief

If self-belief is a problem:

❑ choose projects where an indifferent outcome will not matter to anyone but you
❑ promise yourself that you will not show the work to anyone
❑ work on small projects, short enough for you to be able to suspend self-doubt
❑ when working *pretend* that you are very capable—just as an experiment. It's amazing what you can accomplish when you don't know what you can't do.

You must give yourself permission to turn on your capabilities. Then, even if you don't produce a standard that would leave the world gasping, at least you have started, enjoyed the process and with practice you can only get better.

Only he who does nothing makes a mistake.

French proverb

FIRST DRAFT

Your first attempt to explore an idea in a concrete form I will call a 'first draft'. It could, for example, be a sketch, a plan, a rough run through or an improvisation. Many people approach this draft in the wrong way because they misunderstand its purpose.

The aim is not to produce work of a nearly presentable standard, which is relatively free of mistakes or inconsistencies. Neither is the aim to impress, either yourself or anyone else. The first draft is an experiment, an exploration. You are playing with the idea to discover its full richness and potential. What opportunities does it provide? What are its possibilities? What are the alternative approaches? You must explore every avenue of the idea. When you have completed the first draft you will pass through an evaluation phase and then on to a second draft. These perspiration and evaluation phases are very different in intent, and almost opposite in mind-set.

Perspiration (drafting)

The aim here is to explore possibilities so as to discover and squeeze out every ounce of merit from your ideas. Only explored hopes can be realised. You boldly attempt to make the ideas respond to your aspirations regardless of difficulty. Especially in the earliest drafts you use the inspiration mind-set: engrossed, enthusiastic and uncritical. You must focus on the realisation of potential, not the avoidance of 'error'.

Evaluation (reviewing the drafts)

We will see in the next chapter that the main aim of an evaluation phase is to review your work critically, noting both its strengths and its weaknesses. This requires an opposite mind-set to the perspiration phase: detached and critical. However, you should be critical only of how the idea has been realised or implemented, not critical of the idea itself in nearly all cases.

It is tempting but fatal to adopt the detached and critical evaluation mind-set during perspiration. The first draft in particular is a rough exploration. If critics are not allowed at rehearsals they are certainly not allowed at the first run through!

> Ivor Cutler the poet and musician says he sometimes feels he is working with a critical raven on his shoulder, peering at everything he does and squawking criticisms into his ear.

Why it's a mistake not to make mistakes

In a draft, mistakes are only a problem if you are trying to avoid them. If you are to explore every avenue of an idea, this will include avenues that turn out to be dead ends. So what? This is the only way to explore. You must expect to try out many more approaches than prove feasible in the end.

Dead ends are not mistakes, they are just bad luck; everything you try can't work. Dead ends and mistakes are the inevitable consequence of an open-minded exploration—treasure them! If there are no clangers in the first draft you are not exploring the idea or the medium anywhere near enough and you will never discover the idea's full potential. Or your own.

A draft wouldn't be a draft if it were perfect. So weaknesses cannot 'spoil' a draft. In any case you are not expected to have faith in a draft, but in the potential of the idea or work you are exploring, in what the draft will become. In any case errors are of little significance. It is important to recognise that in all but a very few media, it is relatively easy to remove weaknesses. You simply produce the next draft without them, though it may of course take a series of drafts and redrafts to achieve this. What is difficult is to realise the full potential of an idea.

You must explore every dead end to be sure you have discovered the best way forward. Many writers, for example, are so unconcerned with fault at this stage that they change their mind about a location half-way through a passage, start in the middle or even at the end of what they are working on, go back on themselves to repeat a description over and over in different ways and so on. If someone else should read this, it would appear to be a meaningless mish-mash, full of stuttering indecision and ludicrous inconsistencies.

Writers who produce such a 'pre-draft' do not edit this to completion. They follow it with a draft proper, starting again from scratch. Knowing this, they feel free during the pre-draft to experiment fully, as they know nothing in it need be used. They see the pre-draft not as a flawed draft which they must coax and polish to completion, but as an exploratory mess which helps clarify their ideas and from which they will be able to lift the odd phrase or two.

How do I know what I think until I see what I say?

E M Forster

It is crucial to free yourself from the timidity which is the inevitable consequence of trying to work without error. If this is a difficulty for you, try such a pre-draft no matter what medium you work in. Try also some of the tools described at the end of this chapter.

In conclusion, the aim of a draft is to explore possibility, regardless of weaknesses.

Perhaps the greatest challenge of creative work is to suspend criticism until it can make a useful contribution. This is not until the evaluation phase. Before this phase the critic-beast must be kept on its chain, or it will devour your ideas at birth, long before they have had a chance to grow to their full potential and so defend themselves. If you unchain your critic too soon, you will never discover what you, or your idea, may have grown into.

Focus on purpose

Doing is not enough. You must do the right thing. This requires that your work is directed by the outcomes of a clarification phase. If you have not yet clarified you should certainly begin doing so while drafting and redrafting.

Keep in mind your intentions or purposes for both the whole and for the part you are working on at the time. This is not easy to achieve, but there are huge gains if you can do it. You will waste very little time, and your work will be concise, powerful, direct and highly focused. For example, the Mini revolutionised the concept of the saloon car. But it was not just a great idea, it was a great idea ruthlessly implemented. Every aspect of the car, even the orientation of the engine, was radically rethought with a main purpose in mind.

You can only achieve what you want if you implement with what you want in mind.

SECOND AND SUBSEQUENT DRAFTS

Alternate phases of perspiration and evaluation can be used to form a cycle of gradual improvement, producing drafts and redrafts. The redraft could be in the form of an amendment of a previous draft or each new draft could start from scratch. The one you choose will depend to some extent on your medium. It is easy radically to revise a word processed report, but not a watercolour. A common mistake though is only to consider amendment and then be perpetually dissatisfied with your work. Sometimes you just have to tear it up and start again. Experiment with both amended drafts and clean slate drafts.

Before or during each subsequent perspiration phase (redraft) you will need to:

❑ clarify what you are trying to achieve
❑ change the work in positive response to the preceding evaluation phase by increasing strengths and reducing weaknesses
❑ continue to experiment.

It is common to neglect the latter.

Draft after draft may be necessary and setbacks are the norm, not the exception, even for the most gifted. Indeed it is especially true for the most gifted as they often deal with very new and untested ideas.

Creativity has been compared with inching up Mount Olympus. You keep thinking you can see the top, but when you get there, the summit is miles away and there is a gorge in front of you, so you must retrace your steps. The list of highly creative people who have spent literally decades chasing what they came to see as a false trail is awe inspiring. It includes Einstein, Edison and Darwin. What sustained them through these tribulations we will consider in Chapter 11 on motivation. For now it is enough to say that if you are enjoying the journey, you are not unduly upset by a delayed arrival.

Despite the spontaneous childlike appearance of much of Matisse's work, it was always the result of long meditation and many pre-liminaries. Matisse photographed each stage of the creation of his now famous painting 'Pink Nude' (1935). There were 22 versions before he satisfied himself. The end result has an audacious, child-like simplicity and, paradoxically, great spontaneity. If a master like Matisse can take as many as 22 drafts, how many do you need to make?

Creative ideas are not lightning strikes

'Is all this perspiration necessary? If I was really bright I wouldn't have to work so hard would I?' There is an emphatic unanimity among researchers into creativity that the 'it all came to me in a flash and I just had to write it down' view of creativity is a nonsense. Inching up a mountain of any significance takes time, often a surprisingly long time.

In contrast to acres of literature giving examples like that of Matisse's 'Pink Nude' above, there is a handful of claims to the lightning flash phenomenon. But these turn out to be the culmination of years of preparation, even a lifetime's preparation. Samuel Taylor Coleridge claimed that his poem *Kubla Khan* was composed very quickly indeed, in a kind of opium daze, and was published virtually untouched. But subsequent research showed that he actually undertook significant revisions of his original draft, and that his prior readings and writings filled his mind with the images that would coalesce into the poem.

Genius is 1 per cent inspiration 99 per cent perspiration.

Thomas Edison

The claim for the blinding flash of insight is perhaps stronger in areas such as science where a revolutionary concept can be very 'simple'. Yet Crick and Watson who discovered that the shape of the DNA molecule was a double helix, had been working on the problem for years, and were reading about other helix-shaped molecules at the time. As we have seen, Darwin got his idea about evolution from reading Malthus. But he had been studying evolution nearly all his life and it took the better part of the rest of his life to confirm his 'flash' of an idea. The same is true in any field. We have seen how Picasso and Matisse could both work on an idea for months, with many preparatory studies and revisions.

Robert W Weisberg, a highly regarded researcher who studied the work of a number of geniuses, showed that their work evolved, often very slowly, from their previous work and from the work of others. It did not come in a flash. He concluded that even the most gifted people do not use unique thought patterns, they just know how to use these thought patterns better.

Creativity takes time and perspiration is perhaps its most time-consuming component. Once you have started on a project it often feels that creativity consists of alternate phases of perspiration and evaluation, peppered by the odd few moments of 'inspiration' or 'clarification'. The Latin root of the word create is *creare*, which means to grow and that is a useful way of looking at your creative work. You must expect this growth to take time.

Cézanne had to give up painting flowers. He found they 'withered away too quickly.'

PERSPIRATION TOOLS

The main tools during the perspiration phase are the drafts. Redrafts can be amendments of old drafts or 'clean slates'. Each draft or redraft is followed by an evaluation phase as described in the next chapter. Here are some other tools, mainly for those who have difficulty with the perspiration phase. If you don't have this difficulty, you could skip to the mind-set.

Burst

Set aside a predetermined slice of time, say an hour or less. When this time arrives work very hard on the idea with great speed and intensity and with no editing or evaluation at all. 'Live in the present' by focusing exclusively on what you are doing at the time. Concentrate on the positive aspects of the idea and ignore the weaknesses.

This is, in effect, an improvisation on your chosen idea and the inspiration mind-set should be adopted—deeply engrossed, fearless and free. Do not expect to amend this work to anywhere near completion or this will make you too cautious. A burst can be seen as a high focus exploratory draft. After the session you may be able to see a way forward, as well as having generated some useful material.

Scouting party

This tool gets you started on an intimidating piece of work. You abandon for the moment the aim of producing useful material, or of investigating opportunities in an exploratory or first draft. Your sole aim is to explore difficulties or new and daunting

---

techniques. An expedition sometimes has a scouting party which goes ahead to investigate the lie of the land so as to advise the expedition proper which route to take. This tool does the same, as its aim is to make a preliminary investigation of the problems ahead and to suggest a route through.

Simply create an exploratory draft, or a burst, but expect nothing of value to come out of it, except more familiarity with the problems ahead. As nothing of positive value is expected, you feel freer to take on daunting new difficulties uninhibited by unreasonable expectations.

Once you have explored the difficulties, and you feel you can deal with them, then you probably need to carry out an exploratory draft in order to explore the positive aspects of your idea and its potential before doing a first draft.

If this tool does not work you may need consciously to practise technique, or consider work which is less technically demanding—effective but simple work is always preferable to work that is advanced but ineffective.

Parallel development

It is often difficult to know where an idea might lead until you have developed it further. The solution is to develop two or more promising ideas together and then choose later. You can even amalgamate aspects of each into a later draft.

Ignore difficulties

Some work has an obvious and demotivating difficulty associated with it. An architect may have a technical problem with waterlogged ground, a writer may not know how to start his short story or a manager may be daunted by how her workforce will respond to a change she is planning.

The problem with such difficulties is that they disable future development. So ignore them. Leave them until later. The architect can start outlining the design, the writer can start his story in the middle and the manager can begin to plan the change without concern for the difficulties.

In effect you are making use of incubation here. Your subconscious will be working on the difficulty. It is common to find that an idea is suggested by some detail in the work and the solution 'pops into your head' while you are working. Even if this does not happen, it is often much easier to deal with the problem when you have explored the rest of the work in more detail.

Timetables

Writers often advise writing so many words a day, or for so long every day, regardless of the quality of the outcome.

> *Talent is a question of quantity. Talent does not write one page: it writes three hundred.*
>
> Jules Reynard

Deadline

A surprising number of creative people seem to require deadlines before they begin a perspiration phase. They may of course be clarifying, mentally improvising and incubating ideas before making a start. But they may just be putting it off!

> Rossini sometimes wrote his overtures the night before their first performance.

Many creative people feel they get the best out of themselves when they are in a high state of arousal. However, leaving work until the last minute may not be the best way of achieving this. Why not experiment with other ways of achieving arousal as in the following activity?

Arousal

❑ Before you start, do everything you can to make the session enjoyable and convince yourself that you are looking forward to it.

❑ Convince yourself of the work's interest and importance.
❑ Give yourself a a pep talk—remind yourself of occasions when you produced high quality work. Try to recapture the excitement and confidence you experienced after completing this work.
❑ Deliberately aim to become emotionally involved while you work. Don't fail to praise yourself if you do something well.

Try the above activity in conjunction with the tools described below. It also works well in conjunction with the self-belief activity described on the first page of this chapter. Relying on deadlines may be a symptom of a motivation problem, so Chapter 11 on the creative drive may be a help here.

THE PERSPIRATION MIND-SET

Suppose you have had an idea which you really value and that you must entrust to someone else. How would you want them to work on it? To bring your ideas to fruition work must be persevering, uncritical, enthusiastic and responsive. This ensures that your ideas are given every chance and are not abandoned prematurely. You may find this mind-set daunting, and few people achieve it completely, but Chapter 11 on motivation will help you apply it.

Persevering

Quitters never win, and winners never quit.

Thomas Edison was expelled from school at the age of 12 for being educationally subnormal, but has been described as the greatest inventive genius of all time. He invented the gramophone and the electric light, and filed over a thousand other ingenious patents. He failed thousands of times to make light with electricity. But he would not give up. He said he had a huge advantage over his rivals in knowing so many ways that did not work. This was the mind-set that enabled him to find a way that did work!

An expert is a man who has made all the mistakes, which can be made, in a very narrow field.

Niels Bohr

Being new, creative ideas inevitably bring with them difficulties you have not encountered before. It is easy to give up in alarm or despondency. But you need to be dogged, single minded and persistent in order to bring a new idea into fruition.

Many East Asian cultures barely accept the concept of 'talent'. For them 'talent' is the outcome of the individual's effort and persistence, the sum of their lifetime's learning. Research bears this out. The top violin students at the best music academy in Berlin, all in their early twenties, were found to have practised around 10,000 hours in their lifetime. The second-tier students averaged around 7500 hours.

Uncritical

You must work on ideas with absolute conviction and great enthusiasm. A defeatist attitude is self-fulfilling. If you don't believe in an idea you will soon give up on it, so the idea fails because of this lack of commitment, long before any inherent weakness in the idea has proved fatal. Conversely, if you suspend criticism, and remain positive and optimistic, you will keep trying and so are much more likely to overcome the difficulties. Don't work with the critic on your shoulder, his turn comes next and his mind-set is ruinous to perspiration.

Enthusiastic

Coupled with this uncritical acceptance that an idea can be made to work, you must implement the idea with enthusiasm.

In the field of the creative arts it is particularly important to imbue your work with real spirit and power. The arts are about the communication of feelings and the perspiration phase requires deep identification with these feelings.

Consider for a moment great musicians and actors interpreting their parts. They focus intently on the positive aspects of the work. They work with enormous commitment and great emotion. You must interpret your own ideas like this or they will die from lack of conviction. So, even if you are not a per-.formance artist, try in your perspiration phases to work in this same emotional and positive spirit. This will generate many faults and the drafts may need taming during the evaluation phase, but this is a small problem if, in return, you have put real feeling into your work. Enthusiasm alone can make an ordinary or promising idea outstanding.

Responsive

Alternate phases of perspiration and evaluation throw up the inevitable failures and difficulties. There are two responses to these: defeatist or responsive.

Defeatist

Here you assume the failure or difficulty was due to a personal deficiency which you cannot change—'I am just not talented enough'. Or it was due to external circumstances which you cannot change—'I just don't have the tools for this job'. This response leads to the conclusion that you will never get this right or anything in the future that is like it—'I may as well give up, everything's stacked against me'.

Responsive

Here you see a difficulty as a challenge to your inventiveness and a failure as an opportunity to learn. What went wrong here and how could I do better next time? Could I tackle it a different way? Could I improve my skills or technique? Could I avoid this problem by adopting a different strategy? Or should I just try harder for longer? The assumption is that you can get there in the end, it's just a way of working out how. A failed draft is not a failed idea.

In Chinese the word for disaster also means opportunity.

The responsive person looks for factors over which they have some control, for example technique, strategy, approach, circumstances, effort or persistence. And when confronted by a problem, they *change* one of these factors and try again.

If a strategy doesn't work: don't blame the strategy, as it might have worked in different circumstances; and don't blame yourself, as you can't always know what will work in advance, just *change* the strategy. This approach may seem obvious, but we tend not to think of it when things go badly.

But what happens if you have changed all the parameters you can think of, and you have tried hard enough for long enough, and you still have not succeeded? Well, even the most responsive person cannot be successful all the time. And they should certainly not be blamed for trying! Simply conclude that expectations are too high and change to more achievable goals. So, even here, responsive people find something to change and so are successful—in the long run.

Responsiveness works. It is the only functional and emotionally intelligent approach. It has a straightforward philosophy: if you don't like it, change it. Responsiveness is about turning circumstances to your own purpose and advantage; it is pro-active. It is an invariable characteristic of creative and successful people.

In Chapter 11 on motivation I will look at how to maximise your chances of maintaining this positive mind-set, despite the inevitable setbacks. But now it is time to let the critic-beast out of his cage.

9

EVALUATION

An artist steps back to look at a painting in progress, a writer reads over a draft, a business person reviews the implementation of a new system and an actor thinks about how he delivers a particular line. All these are examples of evaluation of work in progress. Like all the icedip phases, evaluation may last anything from a few seconds to many days.

We have seen in earlier chapters that even for the most gifted, creativity requires persistent effort towards incremental improvement. This can only take place if you check effectiveness while you work, so that those aspects found wanting can be improved or removed. This means that creativity requires alternate phases of perspiration and evaluation.

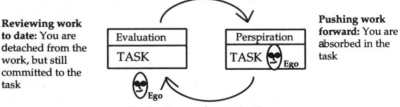

Reviewing work to date: You are detached from the work, but still committed to the task

Pushing work forward: You are absorbed in the task

Evaluation and perspiration

IMPROVEMENT AND LEARNING

This section is loosely based on Kolb's experiential learning cycle. It shows you both how to improve a piece of work and learn from it. The cycle, which you probably follow intuitively to some extent, is shown in the figure below. Then we will illustrate it by an example.

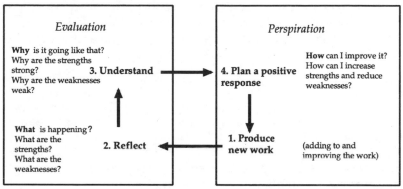

The improvement and learning cycle

Suppose you are a commercial artist designing a CD cover. You **'produce some new work'**, a rough draft, on which you **'reflect'**. You ask yourself how the work is going, and consider its strengths and weaknesses. This should be done in the light of the outcomes of a clarification phase because you cannot know whether a design works, unless you know what it is trying to do. Liking it is not enough. The next two stages of the cycle are often omitted or half-hearted, yet they are crucial to development.

In step 3, **'understand'**, you step up by asking 'Why?' Why is it going like that? Why are the strengths strong? And why are the weaknesses weak? This prepares the ground for improvements of course. But you also learn the general principles of good design, and how to develop your own taste and style. If you know that a design works because it is simple, has strong tonal contrast and an outrageous colour combination, then you can apply these same ideas in an entirely different context to another piece of work. If you don't step up, the effective aspects of your design may remain just a one-off lucky shot.

We learn from our mistakes, but we can learn much more from our successes.

Similarly, if in the **reflect** stage you thought the lettering looked weak, then in the **understand** stage you ask yourself 'Why?' If you come to realise it is weak because there is too much tonal contrast immediately behind it, then you know two things. One is how to put it right, the other is the general principle that you should beware of high tonal contrast behind lettering.

> Creativity researcher D N Perkins studied how poets chose their ideas and found that 'critical appraisals (of ideas) come with reasons for the judgements, rather than reflecting opaque intuitions.'

The next stage is to **'plan a positive response'**. Here you plan how to respond to the previous evaluation and so improve the work as described in Chapter 8 on perspiration. Consider both strengths and weaknesses. You might, for example, decide to make the colour combination even more outrageous (capitalise on strengths) and to reduce the tonal contrast behind the lettering (remove weaknesses). The next draft can then be started ('produce new work') and the cycle repeats. Note that the thinking part of the cycle consists of the questions: 'What?', 'Why?' and then 'How?'

This is a simplified example. In reality your thinking may well be complex and time consuming, unless like many people you miss out stages 3 and 4!

Experience is not what happens to you, it's what you do with what happens to you.

Aldous Huxley

The mentor

Suppose you had an ideal teacher or mentor who supported, guided and encouraged you while you worked, and who entirely understood and valued exactly what you were trying to achieve. How would this angel evaluate your work? In particular, what balance would they strike between a positive or negative response to your work?

Positive	pointing out your strengths praising	showing how the work could be improved	inspiring, encouraging and affirming
Negative	pointing out your weaknesses criticising	reprimanding you for mistakes, errors and omissions	warning and discouraging
Your preferred ratio of positive to negative			

Balancing the positive and negative

Research has shown over and over again that if your work, and your skills, are to develop at their optimum rate your teacher needs to be overwhelmingly positive. Most people would want the teacher to point out opportunities for improvement, but not to be damningly critical about mistakes, errors and omissions. Notice by the way that 'opportunities for improvement' and 'mistakes, errors and omissions' are the same thing, viewed positively or negatively. So there may be no factual difference between positive and negative feedback, but there is always a huge emotional difference. Positive affirmation is the compost of creativity, growing talent, quality, motivation and joy. It also nurtures the self-belief that makes progress possible.

Some people would have their ideal teacher give no negative feedback at all. This is not as dysfunctional as you might think. Researchers observed people learning how to bowl. One group of learners were only told of their strengths, while another group were told only of their weaknesses. Those told only of their strengths improved their bowling very much faster. In many learning situations weaknesses are obvious, and the learner will easily find and correct them unaided if the emotional climate is positive and affirming.

It's decision time. In the table above decide on the ratio of positive to negative that your ideal teacher/friend would adopt. Express it in percentage terms. Would it be 60:40, 80:20 or even 100:0? Choose what you want rather than what you think you ought to choose. As we differ in personality, self-esteem and personal history, we will make different choices here. Write your answers in the box before reading on.

Now I have some good news for you. You have got this ideal mentor and friend already, with you all the time. It is yourself, *if you choose to treat yourself in the affirming and positive way you have just outlined*. Of course you could choose not to treat yourself like this. You could, like most people, choose to evaluate yourself in a very critical manner. But this does not maximise either the improvement of your current work or your rate of learning and development. It cripples both. So why trample on your own future?

It is important to recognise that your evaluation style is a matter of *choice*. Many people are overwhelmingly too hard on themselves during creative work. We live in the age of the cynic, and the cynic's critical and negative mind-set is seen as chic, wise and worldly. Yet the cynic impedes the development growth and self-realisation of both himself and others. Negativity stunts, maims and destroys, and strangles dreams and our own future at birth. It is not easy in our times to adopt the opposite positive and affirming mind-set without a vague feeling that one is being naïve. Yet research is emphatic that only the positive pays.

I am not advocating a flabby and undiscerning 'everything is beautiful' approach. You must admit to and root out weaknesses, and some work is so irredeemably weak that you need to abandon it or start again. But one is rarely in doubt if this is the case. As noted earlier, if the work is new then dead ends and disasters are inevitable, so hardly deserving of censure. Nothing useful was ever created without making a mess first. Weakness, then, is the stage before strength, and does not need condemnation or contempt, but help and encouragement.

It will take time, but try to see evaluation as a safety net that allows your inspiration and perspiration phases to be completely free, an opportunity to be affirming and positive about what works, and as an opportunity to see how to improve what you have done so far—and the way you learn.

Do you evaluate your own work in the ideal way you described in the above table? In our culture emotional states are seen as involuntary, created by external circumstances or by other people. But they do not come from outside; we create them. You can choose to change your emotional reaction to your work if you want to.

Some research suggests that people with an authentic and unquenchable self-belief are more motivated by criticism than by praise, in the short term, but few people involved in creative work have this level of confidence.

Realistic expectations of the quality of your work

One of the hardest aspects of creative work is setting yourself standards to work by. It is important to recognise there are no absolute standards. The very greatest artists in any field often despair at the quality of their work, yet the weakest can be delighted by theirs. When you look at the work of higher fliers, let it inspire you. If you find it depresses you, remember that, however high you fly, there will always be someone flying higher. That is inevitable and irrelevant, and you must forgive yourself for not being the world leader. What does matter is enjoying and benefiting to the full from the skills, abilities and opportunities available to you.

Make your evaluation self-referring. Focus on individual pieces of your work and see how they are better or worse than your own previous work. Set your standards carefully. If your expectations are too high you may give up in despair; if they are too low you may never achieve your full potential. You will grow fastest if your goals for improvement are largely self-referring, challenging enough to inspire you, but attainable in time.

Realistic expectations of the recognition your work gains

Neither are there absolute standards in the recognition you receive, or don't receive, for your work. Even the very highest

---

achievers worry about a fall from grace or how history will judge them. We imagine those we admire in a state of permanent contentment as they bask in fame and admiration. But this is a myth. The facts are that all truly creative people are constantly striving for development, that is their nature. Creative people are happy because they are never content.

Again the trick is not to envy the recognition of others, but to set challenging, yet attainable goals based on your own recognition to date. But you will probably need to sell yourself if you are to achieve this increased recognition.

If you are too keen for recognition there is a danger that you will give unwarranted attention to the opinion of others. You must accept that tastes vary and that many will not understand or appreciate what you are trying to do. It is very dangerous to take any individual criticism to heart, and you must learn to work or laugh it off, unless of course you genuinely agree with it. Remember that evaluations say at least as much about the evaluator as they do about your work

---

Some rejections sent to authors from publishers:
To Samuel Beckett. 'I wouldn't touch this with a barge pole.'
To Stephen King who became a mega-million selling author. 'We are not interested in science fiction which deals with negative utopias, they do not sell.'
To George Orwell (concerning his masterpiece *Animal Farm*). 'It is impossible to sell animal stories . . .'
Of HG Wells ' . . . only a minor writer of no large promise.'
Of Albert Einstein by his teacher. 'this boy will not amount to very much.'

ARE YOU CONFORMIST—OR JUST INFLUENCED?

Social psychologists such as Asch have shown the extraordinary pull of conformity. In one experiment he showed three lines on a card to a group, asking each person in turn which was the longest. It was absolutely clear which was longest. All the members of the group but one, the subject, was an accomplice of the experimenter. Every now and then, all these accomplices agreed that the wrong line was longest. Seventy per cent of Asch's subjects agreed with this blatantly incorrect judgement on at least one occasion.

If people will disbelieve their own eyes in a simple task like this, the tendency to be swayed by majority opinion in matters of taste is almost irresistible. Asch found that the more difficult the judgement, the more this group pressure enforced conformity.

There is nothing wrong with conforming if this takes you where you want to go. Many of the most highly creative people have been conformers, Bach and Raphael for example were not revolutionaries. Instead they 'stood on the shoulders' of decades of brilliant work by other artists and brought the style of their times to its pinnacle. It is not whether you conform, but *why*. If you conform because that is where your heart is, that's fine. If you conform because you have never asked yourself what you are doing and why, or because you want to be accepted, you are not going to fulfil your potential.

To some extent you are lucky if there is some style, school or approach which attracts you. You can then learn a great deal from studying work in this area. Practically all creative people conform to some extent, even if to an *avant garde* school. But you should be clear *why* you conform.

Why are you influenced?

- ❏ Because I genuinely admire the work and opinions which influence me.
- ❏ Because I have never had the chance to sit down and work out my own ideas.
- ❏ Because I can learn from what has gone before.
- ❏ Because conforming to expectations brings financial rewards.
- ❏ Because I would starve if I didn't.
- ❏ Because conforming means my work is more likely to be accepted.

❏ Because there is excellent work by very talented people I want to learn from.
❏ Because I am not talented enough to have my own ideas.
❏ Because there are absolute standards of taste to which my work must measure up.

Which of these reasons is legitimate? The last two certainly are not.

WHO IS EVALUATING?

A crucial issue in the evaluation phase is who has control over the process. You may think for example that you have freely decided something you have done is no good, while in fact you have allowed your critical faculties to be unreasonably influenced. On the other hand, if there is a client who must be satisfied, your critical faculties may not be influenced enough.

Your evaluation of your own work can be client centred, approval centred or truly independent.

Client centred evaluation

If you are a graphics designer or an architect, for example, then you must satisfy your client. But how can you be sure to assess your own work by your client's standards?

First you must interrogate the client to uncover fully their true needs and purposes. The client is rarely fully aware of these, yet will be dissatisfied if they are not met. Key questions are:

❏ Why is the work necessary exactly?
❏ What does the client want to achieve? What are their wants, needs and motives?
❏ What does your client want to avoid and what are their anxieties?
❏ What are the constraints, opportunities and other situational factors?
❏ Is there a hidden agenda? and so on

Even the most detailed brief will not answer these questions, so you will need to talk.

Show the client your portfolio or, much better, ask them to take away a large selection of your work and peruse it in their own time. Ask them to decide which pieces of work they like most and why, and to inform you of this when you next meet. Show them the work of others too, so they get a feel for what the possibilities are. The ideal is that they take this work away to browse through and perhaps discuss with others.

Looking at examples of work like this familiarises the client with possibilities which are obvious to you, but may be an inspiration and a revelation to them. It also helps them to clarify their own goals and needs. You can only satisfy your client if your client is clear of their own goals and you know of these goals. So ask and listen. If the client chooses you after this initial investigation, and they probably will, they will be doing so because they believe you are the most likely to satisfy their needs. If you don't like or can't understand what your client is trying to do, then you have discovered this early and avoided a potentially disastrous working relationship. There is no substitute for starting the relationship with your client with full mutual understanding. This clarification process need not be too time consuming for you, though it might be for them!

Some people manage to resolve the dichotomy between their own and their client's tastes and agendas, by seeing their central creative role as being to satisfy their client. They unselfishly put their skills entirely at the service of those they work for, their own taste being simply irrelevant. This is easier to sustain if there is mutual respect between you and your client.

Will satisfying your clients satisfy *you*? If not, then don't try to pursue your own agenda at your client's expense. This is almost always resented and in the long run it is counter-productive. It is often much better to do personal work as well as client based work and to keep these entirely separate. The personal work may take only a tiny proportion of your time, and may not make any money, but that is not the point as Chapter 11 on creative drive will explain.

Approval centred evaluation

It is natural to seek reassurance, guidance and direction while you learn. But you should learn to develop slowly away from this dependence towards self-evaluation as you become more confident. Many people with plenty of skill find they lack courage in the evaluation phase, tending to edit their ideas so as to conform to the expectations of others. Their own opinions about their work are ill thought out, and easily swamped by their anxiety to impress their audience, or persons of special importance to them. This is a question of degree. We are all influenced to some extent by the opinions of trusted or admired colleagues, of teachers, or of 'gatekeepers' who have the power to decide whether our work is accepted. But many seek at least some degree of independence.

If you are relatively independent of someone's opinion, you will be influenced only when you agree with it. At least sometimes you will disagree with them and reject their advice or evaluation. If you almost never disagree, you may be so anxious for their approval or so unsure of what you are trying to do that you are losing your way.

Being easily influenced is especially common if you have low self-esteem. But everyone needs self-esteem; you can't work without it. So being unduly influenced may be a stage you have to work through while you are finding your self-confidence. Once you begin to feel your self-confidence, try to get out of the habit of depending on the opinion of others. If necessary try to accentuate your idiosyncrasies and uniqueness rather than conforming to expectations. The crucial question is 'Do I think it works?' If you think this is an easy question to answer then you are probably more influenced than you realise.

Are you approval centred?

When you look at your own work in progress are you focused on:

❑ whether it will impress trusted friends or colleagues
❑ how it compares with the work of others

❑ whether you can 'get away with' this or that
❑ trying to make it look as if it were produced by someone you admire
❑ whether it is acceptable to a boss, critic or other important person
❑ protecting yourself from potential criticism by playing safe
❑ whether it will sell
❑ whether it is fashionable or conforming to other widely accepted standards?

Or are you focused on:

* whether it achieves what you set out to achieve
* whether it can better achieve this goal or purpose
* how it compares with your previous work
* learning from its weaknesses and strengths?

Score up to minus four points for every star, and up to plus two for every bullet. An overall positive score is a measure of your approval centredness. Few people score negatively.

The advantages of being approval centred are that you can learn enormously from those with greater skill than you, and the desire for their acceptance creates a strong drive. Working in a recognised way means you will find it easier to get on, and at least some people will understand what you are trying to do. The disadvantage is that you may pay too much attention to approval, and too little to your creative goals and purposes. You will also be less original and authentic than you could be.

Developing truly independent evaluation

If you have sufficient self-esteem about your work, and at least some respect from others for what you have done, you may begin to develop your independent judgement. This is judging your work entirely by your own standards. This will require you to think very deeply about some very difficult questions:

❑ What exactly am I aiming to do with my work and why?
❑ How can this be best achieved in general?
❑ How can this be best achieved in my current piece of work?

Only when you are really clear about these ends can you hope to judge your progress towards them. Though you will probably change your mind about these ends during your career, you should be clear about them at any one time.

It is a commonplace that highly creative people or independent thinkers take risks. This is not, as most suppose, because they all have a reckless nature. It is because they are so driven by curiosity and fascination for their self-made goals that they cannot stop themselves when a risk heaves into view. It is this enthusiasm for their personal goals which gives them both their independent judgement and their dangerous ideas.

Cézanne, for example, had his paintings constantly rejected by the salons in Paris and was brutally criticised when his work was shown in exhibition. One critic wrote that he was 'a sort of madman who paints in *delirium tremens*'. A quiet, sensitive man, he was so mortified by repeated humiliations like this that he withdrew his work from exhibition in Paris for 20 years.

Although his painting was revolutionary he was not a brash iconoclast by nature. He often painted in a three-piece suit, he was very conventional in many respects and desperate for professional recognition. But he had formed a personal view of what painting was and he could not stop himself following it, even if it led to a humiliating rejection by the establishment he admired. Luckily he had a meagre private income that enabled him to continue painting, but what if he had not? And how many talents like this have we lost?

Cézanne, like many creative people, was in part sustained by the high esteem of friends and respected fellow painters whose opinion he valued greatly. Yet such single-minded pursuit of self-selected goals and standards is incredibly rare. If you wish to develop independent judgement you must learn to develop and value your own vision and spirit, and to return to it at times of difficulty. If others think you are mad—you are in excellent company.

> Critics cannot take away your self-respect if you do not entrust them with it.

This advice is notoriously difficult to follow. The pressure to seek approval is enormous and it is so much more agreeable to be liked than to be right. It is also much easier to accept received opinion, than to think things out for yourself!

> Experts on creativity are emphatic about the importance of this independence of mind. Creative people are not trying to 'do it right' using other people's goals and standards, but to 'do the right thing' using their own goals and standards. C R Rogers wrote that the creative person must retain an 'internal locus of evaluation'. (Not a desire to be rich and famous by satisfying the tastes of others!)

Do you remember the 'trust your own taste' activity on page 65? Creativity requires your vision and your judgement at the very centre—not because you are right and the critics wrong, but because you know what you hope to create better than anybody else and you have a right to follow that dream. Others will not agree with you, but that is inevitable and an irrelevance.

Better to write for yourself and have no public, than write for the public and have no self.

Cyril Connolly

It is exciting to set a unique and innovative course. But the dangers are that you will try to do this too soon, before you have clarified personal goals, before you have done your apprenticeship, and when you could still learn much from talking your work over with friends and colleagues. You run the risk of attention seeking by producing cranky, incomprehensible work.

Many highly creative people choose not to become independent. Some take opinions from almost anyone, while some only take them from a trusted group of friends. Many people use a mix of client centred, approval centred and independent evaluation, depending on the context. Whom will you listen to?

PERSPIRATION AND EVALUATION: COMPLEMENTARY OPPOSITES

Perspiration is forward looking, you are engrossed in detail and you must have the confidence, even the arrogance, to take risks as you stretch towards your imaginative vision of what might be. But it is crucial to appreciate that this arrogance or confidence should not be in the work as it stands, but in your vision of what the work can become. It is this confidence in the future which keeps you driving forward.

> The pessimist knows that the egg cannot fly. The optimist can see that it will.

Evaluation of work in progress, however, is backward looking and asks whether your present work realises your vision. It is detached and critical about this work, but should remain absolutely committed to the vision itself and to your ability to realise it. It is very important to keep in mind this crucial distinction between 'what might be' and 'what is'. It is the latter on which your evaluation is concentrated.

It is not reasonable to evaluate a vision until it has been realised, so remain committed to it until you do. Neither is it reasonable to evaluate your capability until it has had a few chances to show what it can do, so remain committed to that, too. This positive thinking is self-fulfilling. If you believe you can do it, you probably will. (As you saw in Chapter 4.)

Perhaps the greatest mistake is to criticise your own 'talents' or skills on the basis of unsuccessful work. Would you evaluate a tennis player solely on the basis of the strokes he or she missed?

Another difference between perspiration and evaluation is that in perspiration you can easily become too engrossed in detail, while during evaluation you 'stand back' to take an overview of the work as a whole. This is why your assessment of a piece of work is so often so very different during the perspiration and evaluation phases. You can depress yourself in a struggle with minute difficulties, only to step back to see that the work seen as a whole is much better than you thought. Or you can be exhilarated in your success at overcoming detailed difficulties only to 'stand back' to see that the overall shape of the work is not right. Clarification and evaluation during perspiration can help to avoid this latter problem, but probably only to some extent.

The purpose of evaluation is to make you reflect on what you are trying to achieve, as much as to help you decide whether you have achieved it in the particular case you are considering.

Perspiration	Confident, even arrogant about the vision	forward looking: focused on realising what might be	engrossed in the work in progress	tends to be focused on detail	In both you are **committed to the vision of what might be and your ability to realise it**
Evaluation	Humble about how the vision has been realised	backward looking: focused on evaluating what is	detached from the work in progress	focused on the big picture and whether the detail realises it	

Perspiration and Evaluation: complementary opposites

Our business in life is not to succeed, but to continue to fail in good spirits.
Robert Louis Stevenson

Success is overrated. Everyone craves it despite daily proof that man's real genius lies in quite the opposite direction. Incompetence is what we are good t: it is the quality that marks us off from animals and we should learn to revere it.

Stephen Pile, *Heroic Failures*

EVALUATION TOOLS

Incubation

As you will see it is useful to leave a day or so between completing a draft and evaluating it.

Parallel versions and parallel edits

You can fork development by allowing two parallel, alternative versions of a work. You can either make two completely different versions of the work as a water-colour artist might do or 'edit' one version in a different way to make a second version as a novelist might do. Word processors make it easy to have, say, a heavily cut and a lightly cut version of the same chapter.

Keeping the original version makes you feel safe while you experiment with daring cuts to a second.

Of course you don't need to keep the parallel versions going forever; you can abandon one of them when you are sure which is best.

Stepping through the design

An architect might imagine someone using their design for a house, doing the washing, making tea for people in the garden and so on. Computer software designers are taught to imagine someone using their programme step by step. They try to consider every eventuality. Whenever possible a real 'road test' is obviously best. I once had a teapot which poured very badly and fell over when you opened the hinged lid to put the tea-bag in. It's surprising how few designers test their designs.

Culling

There is a tendency to be reluctant to cut work you have been working on because you don't want to lose its good qualities. But it is often necessary to be ruthless and to clear away the non-essentials so that the main idea shines through clearly. You can see the main idea, of course, but will others? They are more likely to be dazzled by secondary factors or irrelevant detail.

If you can, consider parallel versions, keeping the more complicated version while working on a cut or simplified version. The latter often turns out to be best.

> When in doubt—leave it out. Raymond Carver said that if his first draft of a story was around 40 pages, it would be half that by the time he was through.

Abandoning a draft

While it is dispiriting to abandon work that you find wanting, it is a universal experience for all involved in creative work. An actor friend tells me he usually abandons three or four attempts at a new character, but usually retains at least one insight from each of the abandoned attempts in his final characterisation. You always learn something from abandoned attempts even if it is only what does not work.

Everyone experiences cycles of optimism and pessimism, as you work towards completion and, like an athlete, you must develop the ability to work through the 'pain barrier' of finding a draft wanting. My photographer brother tells me that when an evaluation is very negative he always goes back to a clarification phase.

> *The vital accessories to my work are my reference books, such as the complete Shakespeare and a prayer book, and a large refuse bin.*
>
> Beryl Bainbridge (in interview)

> *A good writer, in my experience . . . does not write a large number of books but works back over the first one and gets it more or less right.*
>
> Malcolm Bradbury

Bottom drawer

If you are making very small changes, are they making very big differences? Some find it hard to say 'it's finished', partly because they fear the criticism that might follow the remark. Remember to trust your own taste and judgement. If you think it's done—it's done. Others usually notice what you have got right and what you take for granted, while you can be too closely tuned to tiny details that others simply won't notice.

Finish the work in draft form if you can, then put it 'in the bottom drawer'. Begin working on something else. When you go back to it again later you will see it afresh, and both opportunities for improvement and the final judgement become much easier.

THE EVALUATION MIND-SET

In order to evaluate work produced during a perspiration phase you need to be *critical*, *positive* and *willing to learn*. This is a difficult mix.

Critical

We have seen that you must sustain an honest humility about the quality of the work to date, while maintaining an arrogant confidence about both what the work will become and your ability to get it there. You must distinguish between what might be and what is, and only criticise the latter.

Every book is the wreck of a perfect idea.

Iris Murdoch

How and what you criticise is crucial. You must maintain your sense of purpose when evaluating your work. You should not just be asking 'Do I like it?, but 'Is the work taking me where I want to go?' Frequent periods of clarification will help.

To be honest and effective in your criticism you must detach your ego from your work. Don't be defensive, it is the draft work you are criticising *not yourself or your vision*. It is as though someone else did the work for you, and you are deciding whether it comes up to your standard, and whether it does what you want.

You must have a no-blame policy about the mistakes and disasters you find. If failures are inevitable, they are hardly blameworthy. So your ego, rather than being attached to your work, must be attached instead to the vision of what the work will become. It must be confidently urging you towards what might be.

You can't make a Hamlet without breaking a few egos.

William Goldman (screenwriter)

Positive

For most people evaluations need to stress the positive; this maximises both improvement of the work and your learning. This aspect of the evaluation mind-set is notoriously difficult as there is a natural tendency for deficiencies and weaknesses to shout down the strengths. You must celebrate the positive aspects of the work, as well as see its weaknesses, or you will lose your enthusiasm and motivation.

The balance between the critical aspect of the evaluation mind-set and the positive aspect is vital and difficult. Remain in control of your emotional reaction to your work. If you have problems, abandon the critical entirely and concentrate on the positive.

Willing to learn

Humility about progress to date enables you both to improve the work and your own skills. Very capable people often know themselves to be fallible, indeed that's how they became capable in the first place. They corrected their mistakes and learned from them, instead of pretending they got it right first time.

If your ego is too strongly attached to your work, you will resent criticism, so you will stunt your own and the work's progress.

> The portrait painter Sir Godfrey Kneller was massively conceited, genuinely believing that the world would have been a better place had God consulted him at the Creation. With an attitude like that was he likely to improve?

An evaluation phase often looks forward into the next perspiration phase. In particular, you must be ready to think responsively. What can you change to avoid the weaknesses you have found? How can you build on your strengths?

It is always fatal to confuse the near opposite mind-sets for perspiration and evaluation. If you evaluate with enthusiastic arrogance, your work will never improve and you will not learn. If you work in a critical and detached manner, you will soon give up. You must carefully monitor your mind-set during these phases and ensure you are using the correct one.

INCUBATION

Don't just do something—sit there!

The French mathematician Henri Poincaré tells of how he discovered a general equation for 'Fuchsian functions'. He had been
working on the problem for some time with little success. Then
he set off on a journey to a conference on an entirely unrelated
matter. He had forgotten entirely about his mathematical work,
when he stepped on to a bus . . . 'Just as I put my foot on the
step, the idea came to me, though nothing in my former thoughts
seemed to have prepared me for it.' He had the solution, yet it
bore no relation to his former work on the matter, and he wasn't
even thinking about the problem at the time.

You may well have had a similar experience where, after
days of conscious striving have failed, an elegant solution floats
effortlessly into your mind a few days later. The solution is
typically quite unlike any path you have tried consciously. The
unconscious seems to think laterally, often taking the conscious
mind by surprise with the unexpectedness of its ideas, as well
as by the arbitrariness of the time of their arrival.

Many of the greatest minds testify to such an experience:
Archimedes, Newton, Pasteur, Columbus, Edison, Fleming,
Nobel . . . It seems that the very pinnacle of conscious thought,
science and mathematics, often progresses by means of the
unconscious.

The mind is like an iceberg; we are directly aware only of the
part that floats above the level of consciousness. Many of us
ignore the huge power of the unconscious, even though it regu-

lates all the immensely complex functions of our body. It fights off infections and replaces worn-out cells without conscious help. It has access to memories not accessible to the conscious mind and all our learning. And in mental illness, the unconscious can completely overcome the conscious mind. Yet we often ignore it.

Artists, however, seem unanimous and emphatic that creative work involves the unconscious. Jung was perhaps the chief architect of this idea. He and other psychiatrists have shown that the unconscious is the seat of our conflicts, urges and anxieties, and the origin of our most profound and extreme emotions, both positive and negative. It seems likely that art is the process by which unconscious and subconscious ideas of deep emotional significance are given conscious expression, whether this is for example sexual passion, love of nature, childhood obsessions or the abhorrence of war. The best art explores and expresses these passions, and can give us a better understanding of them, and so gives meaning to the most important aspects of our lives. Art seems to be the way our psyches communicate.

Whether we are an artist or, like Poincaré a problem solver, we must make peace with the invisible and prodigious force of our unconscious. We must find a way of tapping this most capable and potent ally. But how?

> Whenever Sir Isaac Newton had a particularly thorny problem he always worked on it just before he went to sleep, reporting that, 'I invariably woke up with the solution'.

First you could simply give yourself a break from the work and allow yourself a period of incubation. This is a particularly good idea after an inspiration phase, or a perspiration phase, and before an evaluation phase. But incubation is also helpful if you are experiencing difficulty within a phase, especially clarification or evaluation.

Too many potential creators are inhibited by a belief that gifted others solve problems directly

D T Campbell (on scientific discovery)

A period of incubation has a number of advantages:

❑ It gives your unconscious mind time to work. Many psychologists believe that during incubation your unconscious is actively searching for useful material, in particular for analogies of the present problem or difficulty.

❑ If you ponder your problems from time to time during the incubation phase it will also give your conscious mind time to solve the knottier problems. Deep thought, especially clarification, is often more effective when you are not impatient for progress with your pencil itching in your hand. If you relieve yourself from the pressure to produce, if you disengage and look at things in perspective and from different angles, the way ahead often becomes clearer.

❑ It allows your ego to disengage from your work. If you have put a little distance between yourself and your ideas to date, you will evaluate them more honestly.

❑ The role of the fortunate accident in creative work is often underestimated. If you carry a problem around with you for a day or so, something you come across may be fruitfully related to your work. Newton was trying to work out what force made the moon keep to its orbit about the earth when the apple was said to have fallen on his head. Then he had it, gravity was the force he was looking for. He is not the only one to benefit from a lucky accident to a prepared mind.

RELAXATION AND CREATIVITY

When I feel well and in a good humour, or when I am taking a drive or walking after a good meal, or in the night when I cannot sleep, thoughts crowd into my mind as easily as my mind might wish.

Wolfgang Amadeus Mozart

Is it possible to tap the unconscious in a deliberate way? Mozart's account above gives us an insight born out by modern research.

Electro-encephalographs (EEGs) have been used by researchers to make 'brain waves' visible. Four main types of brain wave have been isolated, each associated with different mental states.

β : **Beta waves:**
about 12–25 cyles per second

Beta waves are characteristic of the conscious mind when it is wide awake, alert and working.

α : **Alpha waves:**
about 9–11 cycles per second

Alpha waves are slower, and are found during relaxation, meditation, daydream or reverie. This is a state of relaxed alertness which is thought to facilitate intuition and inspiration, because it allows contact with the subconscious. **Theta** waves are even slower at 4 to 8 cycles per second. They are produced during deep meditation, or when close to sleep, and again some commentators link these waves with creativity. **Delta** waves are made in deep dreamless sleep.

> Jung believed that in our 'collective unconscious' we have archetypes, symbols and myths, each with a potent emotional charge, and that these are crucial to the communication of artistic ideas.

This is the benefit of 'sleeping on it'. The slower brain waves of relaxation and sleep seem to give the subconscious an opportunity to contribute creative ideas to the conscious mind. Though continual periods of concentrated effort generate ideas and force progress, periods of reverie, rest and sleep between them are vital to problem solvers and to creative artists. They allow you to tap that fathomless and powerful ally, your unconscious. You can make deliberate use of reverie as explained in Chapter 4 on inspiration.

Many creative thinkers take intermittent walks when working on knotty problems. Darwin had a special circular path created in his garden for this purpose. Adequate oxygen intake is important for optimum brain function. Also, walking gives you time to ruminate in a relatively relaxed, 'alpha wave' manner.

As a sick child Descartes was allowed to spend as much time as he liked in bed. When he grew up he continued the practice, saying it was the best place to think.

MAKING USE OF INCUBATION

Incubation is easy. Finish the previous session by reviewing your current work so it becomes clear in your mind. This includes any inconsistencies, half-baked ideas or unresolved problems. Don't be anxious about these, they are inevitable after all; trust yourself to find the solutions. If you can, frame a clear statement of what you need in order to proceed. 'I need a way to . . .' Then put the work out of your mind in an optimistic, 'I know I can sort this out' frame of mind.

Ponder the problem in a playful way from time to time, but concentrate on other things. When you go to bed, hold your current work and any problem lightly in your mind. Try making use of reverie. When you wake in the middle of the night or in the morning, try again a playful tussle with the difficulties. Be receptive to silly or half-wakeful ideas or approaches. If the solution doesn't come, just say to yourself that it will eventually. It is fatal to force the pace. Don't dismiss incubation because the problem is not solved overnight. You must trust rather than try.

Some contend that the language of the unconscious is that of imagery, symbols and dreams, and that it often does not communicate with the conscious mind directly. Psychiatry certainly bears this out. Professor David Fontana in *The Secret Power of Dreams* suggests that dreams can be used to solve problems. I have never experienced this myself, but have often had very useful ideas after half waking in the middle of the night.

However, there is plenty of anecdotal evidence and some research to support Fontana's thesis. He suggests that during a period of incubation you use word association on any images encountered in dreams to discover any relation between your dream and your creative work. You will need to be patient and to persist over many nights.

The Russian chemist Mendeleev dreamed the periodic table of the elements so accurately that only one value in the complex table needed to be changed.

The ring structure of benzene came to Kekulé in a reverie where his conscious mind watched imaginary atoms moving before his eyes. Eventually one snake-like chain of atoms seized hold of its own tail. Kekulé awoke from his reverie with a start, realising at once that this was the unique form of the benzene molecule.

Otto Loewi dreamed a highly ingenious experiment to show that nerve impulses were chemical as well as electrical. The experiment worked and he got a Nobel prize for it in 1936.

Revelations like the ones above only occur to the 'prepared mind', that is, one that has worked very extensively on the problem.

INCUBATION TOOLS

If it is difficult to forget, try working on your next project or on some entirely unrelated work. The other tools for incubation have been described above. You might, though, like to make use of reverie as described on page 53 and random association by accident as described on pages 53–6 during incubation. But you should only do this very occasionally in a playful way.

THE INCUBATION MIND-SET

'Sleeping on it' is the universal advice when you are involved with difficult thinking. But it is not always easy advice to follow.

In order to adopt a period of incubation you must be *unhurried, trusting* and *forgetful*.

Unhurried

You must be prepared to accept that there is a limit to what conscious thinking can achieve. Often the struggle and strife of perspiration and inspiration can only get you so far, and there is no option but to give up for the time being. You cannot force the pace of creative work and anxiety about deadlines will be counter-productive if it makes it difficult for you to 'forget' your work.

Trusting

You will not cease striving unless you trust incubation to find a way forward. Only your successful use of incubation will give you this trust. Some creative people are so struck by the quality of ideas provided by incubation, and their sudden and unexpected arrival, that they believe the ideas come from a greater power than themselves, from God or from a muse. Incubation is not a special facility, everyone experiences the benefit of sleeping on it.

Forgetful

Now what was that I was working on?

Part III

Creativity and motivation

FINDING THE CREATIVE DRIVE

YOUR FIVE 'GO' BUTTONS

The psychologist Abraham Maslow showed that we have just five instinct-like needs:

intrinsic motivation

Self-actualisation needs:
the need to fulfil one's abilities and talents. To follow one's own nature to become idiosyncratically oneself

Esteem needs:
to be respected by others and to have self-esteem

extrinsic motivation

Belongingness and love needs:
to give and receive affection, and to be accepted by a group

Safety needs:
security, and freedom from death, injury or debilitating poverty

Physiological needs:
food, air and water etc

growth

Maslow showed that if you are fortunate enough to have a lower need largely satisfied, then it tends to diminish as a motivating factor for you, but is then replaced by the next higher need and so on. Most people are only partly satisfied in the top three needs, but one is often predominant.

These needs are your 'go' buttons, in fact you are likely to be involved in creative work because it satisfies at least one of these needs. For example, a designer who is mainly motivated by belongingness and love needs may concentrate on being accepted as 'one of the gang' in the design office. A colleague who is mainly motivated by esteem needs will concentrate on getting respect for his work and a sense of self-esteem from succeeding in challenges. A self-actualising designer may focus on the intrinsic nature of the task, and how she thinks this should be approached. Being largely satisfied in the lower needs they become less important for her, so for example she may be prepared to take criticism from others in the team without fearing rejection or suffering a blow to her self-esteem. Entirely self-actualising people are very rare.

Most people are motivated by a mix of these needs. In what proportion do they motivate you? Your answer can depend on context. You may be self-actualising with personal work and focused on esteem needs at the office. How you are motivated greatly affects how you work and how you evaluate your work. However, up to a point you can change this if you want to.

SELF-ACTUALISATION AND INTRINSIC MOTIVATION

Since I reached the conclusion that the essence of the creative person is being in love with what one is doing, I have had a growing awareness that this characteristic makes possible all the other personality characteristics of the creative person: courage, independence of thought and judgement, honesty, perseverance, curiosity, willingness to take risks and the like.

Paul Torrance, creativity researcher

. . . no one has ever enjoyed science as much as Einstein.

V John-Steiner

Exceptionally creative people are very often involved in a labour of love. For them the task is an end in itself, not a means to an end. They may be driven by curiosity, fascination or a vision of the future, or by a passionate need to articulate their feelings in some artistic form. Their motivation is their love of the task. This is *intrinsic* motivation. At least while they are working, such concerns as whether their work will be well received critically, or whether it will earn them much money, are blotted out by their obsession with the task itself. This gives them that daring, risk-taking independence of mind which is so characteristic of creative people.

Alternatively, one may perform a task not for its own sake, but because it might eventually provide rewards such as money, fame, promotion, beating the competition or critical acceptance. Such motivation, coming from outside, is called *extrinsic* motivation. It is external to the task itself.

Do not assume that a hobbyist is necessarily intrinsically motivated; they may be obsessed with winning a competition, or by impressing their teacher or friends. Equally, a commercial artist may so enjoy his work that there is nothing he would rather do, so he is intrinsically motivated. Most of us operate somewhere between these two extremes, but we have the power to change our position on this continuum as you will see.

The quality of work produced has been found to be exceptionally sensitive to whether the individual sees the task as having intrinsic or extrinsic value. Let's look at the two extremes of intrinsic motivation (labour of love) and extrinsic motivation (means to an end) separately. Then we will see how to move ourselves towards the more productive intrinsic motivation.

Much of what follows will surprise you. It may seem hard to accept in this hard-bitten and materialist age, but research in this area seems emphatic and it has immense relevance whether you work for pleasure or in an uncompromisingly commercial environment.

In a long series of carefully controlled experiments Hennessey and Amabile asked groups of children and adults to perform precisely the same task (making a collage) but for different reasons. Some groups were asked to do it for reward (extrinsic motivation), while others were offered no reward (intrinsic motivation). The originality, creativity and persistence of those who were not rewarded was much greater.

The researchers suggest that the reward devalued the task itself, and the threat of external evaluation made subjects more self-conscious and less risk-taking. They found that the subjects' subsequent enjoyment of the task was reduced even after the rewards were removed and the researchers had gone.

Intrinsic motivation—Labour of love

If you are driven by *pure* intrinsic motivation you enjoy the work for its own sake, so you will tend to maximise both the effort and the time you spend on the task. I mean here a self-chosen task which exactly matches your interests and aspirations, there is nothing else you would rather do and you are doing it for love.

Your level of concentration will be high and you will be indulgent of any difficulty, seeing it as a fascinating challenge rather than a frustrating impediment to your hopes. Some scientists and academics, for example, have spent a lifetime in the passionate pursuit of a goal they never met, yet they died very happy because it was the fascination of the journey they craved, not the honour of arrival.

Such highly motivated effort is likely to generate at least some success and the virtuous circle shown below is developed, along with an increase in self-belief.

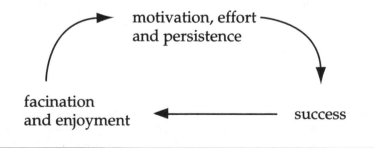

This is enough in itself to render intrinsic motivation important, but that is not all.

You are so absorbed in such tasks that you are entirely engrossed, living in the 'here and now'. Consequently you are unselfconscious, even self-forgetful, which more or less guarantees the individual voice, originality, playful risk-taking, and the sincerity which is so characteristic and so highly prized in creative work. Also, if your sole aim is to please yourself, then you are likely to be independent and self-confident in your taste and judgement.

The work you produce will certainly be of the highest quality you are capable of, but not necessarily of a high quality compared to the work of others. But this does not matter to you because it is the doing you enjoy, the learning and the exploring, not the product. Amateurs are often maligned for the low standard of their work, yet it is a great strength to do a task for enjoyment's sake and a weakness to work hard only to impress others.

You will tend to be interested in tasks that have engaged you for some time and for which you probably have a special aptitude. This enables you to draw on what a painter friend calls 'a lifetime's obsession'. If you have such a passion everything related to it is remembered, you seek out related experiences, the exhibitions, books and everyday observations which feed it. Enthusiasts have a ravenous appetite for anything related to their interest and even trivia is remembered for a lifetime. All this is stored away in the long-term memory and in the unconscious or subconscious. So you are tuned to your task in the most precise way possible.

If a task holds such a fascination for you the quality of concentration you can sustain can be enormous, so large in fact that you can work for hours in unselfconscious immersion. We have all experienced this to some degree, even if only as a child in play. Creativity is, in a sense, the adult at play. But just as play is hugely developmental for children, so is creativity for adults. A task of intrinsic interest gives you a chance to grow in a chosen direction and in a field which you value above all others. You are growing, fulfilling your unique potential and fascinations, discovering your unique interests and style, making your unique contribution in a task so minutely tuned to your individual passions, skills, taste and talent that no one could do it quite like you. This is soul surfing, and it is one of the most privileged and fulfilling experiences in life. Many consider it a near spiritual experience. This is what you are here for. You are exploring, and so finding and fulfilling your life's mission. You have *made* a 'meaning' for your life.

Such immersion is unlikely to come to you unless you have found an activity you genuinely enjoy doing for its own sake and for your own reasons. Then in time this interest will often develop into an enthusiasm and then a passion. We tend to associate this 'flow' with inventing, scientific discovery, playing an instrument, painting or writing. But it is one of the triumphs of the human spirit that this 'soul surfing' is not an experience for the privileged few and is not restricted to artistic or academic activities. I know people who experience it while running a business, campaigning for social reform, building follies, training horses, maintaining motorcycles and growing vegetables in a tiny garden.

Many people do not explore tasks of intrinsic interest because they feel guilty about 'wasting' time on such pursuits. They feel much happier earning money, going to the supermarket or fixing the shower. But such activities merely provide for our material needs. Then we are ready—but ready for what? Is the entire purpose of life to maintain our existence?

> The common housefly has been found to spend 60 per cent of its time performing necessary functions such as eating, resting and finding a mate. The rest of its time it has to itself. What percentage of your time do you have for yourself?

Extrinsic motivation

At the other extreme, if you are involved in a creative activity which is extrinsically motivated, then by definition the reward is more important than the task. Your focus shifts from the task to the reward and who is in control of this. This reward might be the praise of your teacher or friends, the applause of an audience, your boss's approval or the client's pay cheque.

You are mindful of whom you must impress, of the acceptability of what you do in the mind of the reward giver. You take fewer risks, you explore less, you trust your own taste less. You may economise your effort, adopting a 'good enough' approach, and do only what is necessary. You are end focused, eager to have it over and short tempered with difficulties which delay gratification. Your subconscious and unconscious are unlikely to get involved, your spirit is absent and you are less likely to be tuned to the task. There is little sense of self-expression, self-discovery or growth.

I have considered the extremes here and in the real world most of us operate somewhere between them. Some corner of our lives, though, should be left to explore entirely intrinsic interests, as we shall see.

Becoming more intrinsically motivated at work

The real world requires that you respond to the constraints of your situation, and to the expectations of others, but you must regard this only as the starting point if you wish to increase your intrinsic motivation. Within these constraints there will be opportunities for you to take control of the situation so that you can meet self-defined goals and purposes. You must ask yourself:

> 'What do I think is most important?'
> 'What do I get most enjoyment from in my work?'
> 'What do I want to achieve here?'

If you work with others these self-defined goals may be related to your role or to you personally. For example Katrina, a graphics artist, asked herself the above questions and answered as follows:

I think its most important to:

❑ value the client and involve him in my work, right from draft to completion
❑ recycle waste paper and adopt environmentally friendly practices.
I find most enjoyable:
❑ having a really attractive working environment
❑ learning from other people's work in the studio.
I want to achieve
❑ a strong and loyal client base which values my work
❑ an improvement in my airbrush technique.

Katrina can meet the extrinsic requirements of her job *and* achieve these personally defined goals, *but only if she has thought these out and set them as targets for herself.*

Once she has decided on these intrinsic goals, Katrina will probably work differently. She may reorganise her workspace to make it more attractive, cultivate her clients more assiduously and be more deliberate about learning from her colleagues.

If these are really the most important goals for Katrina, then placing emphasis on these 'intrinsic objectives' will make her happier, more fulfilled, more productive and more creative. Notice that most, or arguably all, of her intrinsic objectives are in line with likely company objectives. This is usually the case for all but the most alienated of employees.

To increase intrinsic motivation and make your work more meaningful, fulfilling and enjoyable, you must examine your own goals, values and purposes. You must step up the thought—action continuum to the very top, and ask yourself what you value and enjoy, what you see as the purpose of your work. This requires very deep thinking—these questions are hugely challenging. But the process of answering these ultimate questions is inspiring and liberating. So is working towards the goals they uncover.

It is important to appreciate that only what you value can really inspire you. Your values are your ultimate purposes and your ultimate motivators. Fulfilling other people's agendas is only likely to inspire you if they happen to be in line with your own, though you can of course satisfy your esteem needs through such work.

So to increase intrinsic motivation and creativity, you must discover what is most important for *you* in creative work and work towards these ends.

Intrinsic motivation and management style

The management style you work under has an enormous influence on the extent to which you are likely to become intrinsically motivated. The crucial factor is whether management is *controlling* or *trusting*. Again I will take extremes to illustrate my point.

Suppose you are controlled and not valued at work, condemned to passively act out a role dictated by others, with no real say in how your work is done. Implicit in such a high level of control is a lack of trust in you as a person. Your manager is saying in effect that you do not have the abilities, the ideas or the character to be able to do the job without detailed guidance and surveillance. Such a job is likely to be predictable and there is little of you in it. In time you are likely to feel frustrated, devalued and powerless, and your self-esteem falls. You suffer a loss of zest for life and for work.

You may blame yourself, and feel despairing and dejected, or you may think 'that's life', and become fatalistic and withdrawn. Alternatively you may resent the management style and become alienated, obstructive or even hostile. Whatever your reaction, your motivation falls and yet more control is required to make you do the job satisfactorily, causing a vicious circle. Close approximations to this extreme case are not uncommon in British, French or US industry.

The opposite approach is for the management to inspire your creative action through openness, respect and trust. (This approach is quite common in Germany and Japan.) Again taking the extreme case, instead of controlling, the manager delegates almost entirely to you the responsibility for the implementation of your job description, allowing you as much freedom as possible to approach the job in the way you think fit. Management are open about their difficulties and fears, bringing you into their confidence. They ask you for your opinion about matters related to your job and about the firm in general. They listen to your reply and give it weight. They commonly praise your work when it merits it and may even show an interest in you as a person, seeing you as someone with more than just an economic value.

Your management make clear how important your job is, mainly by showing genuine appreciation when you do it well. You find the job demanding and interesting, you feel real responsibility for what you do and you have a genuine sense of identity within the organisation. You are stretched, so you learn and grow. Your self-esteem rises significantly, as does your motivation. You are likely to be committed and loyal. You enjoy the work and feel a need to do the job well.

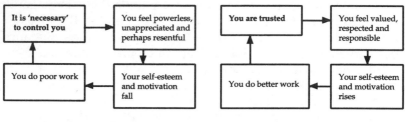

Controlling management style   Trusting management style

Controlling versus trusting management

Clearly it is much easier to set intrinsic goals for yourself in this trusting management system than in the controlling one. However, you can take some control in any working situation by setting intrinsic objectives for yourself.

If you manage the creative action of others, consider your management style very carefully. There is a tendency to manage others the way you were managed yourself, which may not be appropriate. The trusting management style may seem far fetched to you if you have not experienced it. It is an approach first suggested by the work of people such as Abraham Maslow and Douglas McGregor in the 1950s and 1960s. Research has persistently shown that this style motivates staff far better than the more common controlling style. For example, Jeffrey Feffer, in *Winning with People*, showed that the top ten, long-term, best-performing companies on the US stock exchange all adopted a trusting management style.

The trusting management style will not work immediately by magic. It requires time and patience to establish. Modern developments such as Investors in People, Total Quality Management (TQM) and virtually the whole of modern management theory have adopted this 'trusting' model. As ever though, common practice lags behind best practice by some decades.

Intrinsic motivation outside work

Again you must start by stepping up the thought–action continuum to the very top with those daunting but fascinating questions:

> What do I think is most important in my (creative) work?
> What do I most enjoy in my work?
> What am I trying to achieve with my work?

Again there will be extrinsic controlling factors such as financial or time constraints. Like Matisse (see page 116) you must find your way around these as best you can by keeping your true purposes in mind. There will also be your self-esteem needs to satisfy. But try to focus on:

❏ **Your own agenda** not the fulfilment of other people's agendas or tastes
❏ **Controlling the situation** not letting the situation control you
❏ **Opportunities** not extrinsic constraints, problems or difficulties
❏ **Making life worth living** not being content simply to preserve it.

In short you must focus on intrinsic goals as explained above and on page 113.

Of course it is one thing to have intrinsic goals and quite

another to meet them. For this you need two magic ingredients: hope and self-belief. I say 'magic' very deliberately because hope and self-belief have been shown to be self-fulfilling even when they are entirely groundless.

Researchers Rosenthal and Jacobson deliberately gave teachers false hopes of their pupils. They tested school pupils and pretended to their teachers that they were able to identify pupils whose attainment was about to improve substantially, passing the names of these 'improvers' over to their teachers. In fact the names of these 'improvers' were chosen at random. When the researchers returned a year later objective tests showed that the 'improvers' had indeed improved! The authors showed that the IQs of the 'improvers' had increased significantly in comparison with the IQs of 'non-improvers'. Thus the prophesy, despite having no basis in fact, was 'self-fulfilling'. This research has been repeated successfully many times with adults and with other children.

The 'placebo effect' is another example of the self-fulfilling power of hope. If a doctor gives a patient a chalk tablet telling him that it will lower his blood pressure, then his blood pressure will go down. Doctors have even given patients who were vomiting a drug which actually *encourages* vomiting, while telling them that it will prevent it. The vomiting stopped, despite the action of the drug!

As any sports coach will tell you, the power of self-belief is extraordinary. You have every reason to have unreasonable hopes!

Hope and belief also have an extraordinary effect on the unconscious, a part of the mind with considerable influence over creative work. A hypnotist can touch a subject with a pencil while suggesting that it is a red hot poker and the subject's skin will immediately blister.

As well as being self-fulfilling, the 'magic' powers of hope and self-belief are also self-reinforcing. The more hope you have the more likely you are to be successful, and the more successful you are, the higher your hopes. Of course despair and lack of self-belief are also self-fulfilling and self-reinforcing. If you have no hope you soon give up and say, 'I knew I couldn't do it'.

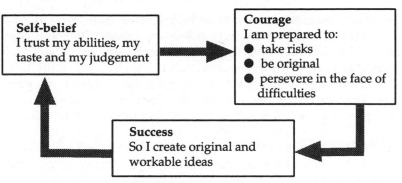

Self-belief, courage and success

Everything created was once a dream, and the annals of creativity groan with the weight of evidence showing that creative people are inspired by personal dreams and then driven by unreasonable hopes. This is the way you make the future take the shape of your aspirations.

CREATIVITY AND GROWTH

My feeling is that the concept of creativeness and the concept of the healthy, self-actualizing, fully human person seem to be coming closer and closer together, and may perhaps turn out to be the same thing.

A H Maslow

Peter works in a dull job, but thinks wood carving is the most satisfying and interesting activity on the planet. When he makes time to do this, he is not simply enjoying himself but valuing himself, he is saying 'What I value matters, because I matter'. It increases his self-esteem and allows him to grow, in an area he considers important, to explore his unique talents and interests.

Some people find meaning and purpose in their lives from outside of themselves, from religion for example. But increasingly people are making their own meaning by following their highest values. Only these intrinsic goals can give meaning and purpose to life. But Maslow also believed we all have an innate and fundamental need to be self-evolving, to grow in the direction of our values, and so discover our individual talents and passions—discover ourselves in fact. Maslow showed that such intrinsically motivated activity was a requirement for full mental health and fitness, as well as a potent motivator for creativity. It is as though growth in the direction of self-defined value is an instinctive human need, which we deny ourselves at our peril. Yet many of us are denied growth opportunities at work, and see creative pursuits as self-indulgent and time wasting at home.

I've always wanted to be somebody, but now I see I should have been more specific.

Jane Wagner

Maslow studied hundreds of 'self-directed' or 'self-actualising' people at home and at work. What did they do? You won't be surprised. They painted, wrote, acted, made things, researched, campaigned, helped others ... In short they indulged themselves in often surprisingly unselfish and constructive activities. The individuals benefited hugely from allowing themselves to do what they saw as most important and often saw this activity as a self-defining vocation or mission. But Maslow points out that their community gained too. Indeed it could hardly survive without their creative drive. Many of these people were at the growing tip of progress in their field, developing the ideas that would shape tomorrow. Others were involved in more everyday activities, teaching, caring, running voluntary organisations or charities, organising entertainment for others ... Self-directed activity is always deeply beneficial to the individual, but is usually beneficial to the community as well, often strikingly so.

Maslow was particularly interested in the ultimate reasons they gave for their self-directed actions. Why does Peter like wood carving? Ultimately because he likes making something beautiful from a natural material. When you ask Peter 'Why?' he can give no answer. Beauty is an ultimate value, it has value in itself, not because it confers a higher order value. By comparison saving money, for example, is not an ultimate value, because you can meaningfully ask, 'why save money?'

Maslow found that the ultimate values motivating free human activity were such ultimate purposes as efficiency, discovery, uniqueness, beauty, truth, justice, growth, peace, happiness and so on.

Man's main task in life is to give birth to himself.

Erich Fromm

Maslow studied primitive societies and showed that, in the most successful, there was a mutually beneficial pact between the individual and the community. The community valued the individual's freedom to act in a self-directed manner, and consequently benefited greatly from both their sense of mental well-being, and the products of their self-actualising labour. So the individual's and the community's quality of life became mutually supporting in a mutually beneficial or 'symbiotic' relationship.

What if your actions are invariably controlled by extrinsic factors? Then you put the needs dictated by circumstance, your lists, your in-tray, in control of your life, and in so doing you show that you value the mundane maintenance of existence and the needs of others more highly than even your most cherished values. You are doing violence to your deepest nature. You devalue yourself, and your life becomes literally value-less, and so goal-less, purposeless. You maintain an existence which has no meaning. There is a loss of self-respect and zest for life, and perhaps a creeping apathy and alienation.

Sadly this is not an uncommon condition in highly industrialised societies. Yet it is rare in successful 'primitive' cultures, because unlike us, they do not see self-denial as an unqualified virtue, but as self-destructive, and because they give more freedom to individuals. They are more trusting, of themselves and of each other. Anthropology shows quite clearly that this trust is self-fulfilling.

If we give ourselves the freedom to explore our potential in the direction of our values then we will grow, gain a sense of purpose and a sense of self, give meaning to our lives, and maximise our creative drive and our usefulness to the communities in which we play and work. These are great rewards.

The artist is not a special kind of man, but every man a special kind of artist.

Eric Gill

missionary
you work exclusively
towards your own
vision

Free

↑

**Intrinsically
motivated:**
- you respond to your
  own vision
- you are creative
  with high motivation

self-fulfilling
(and) you identify your **own**
values and goals, and work
towards these

↑

Proactive
(and) you identify with the
goals you have been set, and
actively work towards them

↑

Reactive
(and) you understand and work
towards the goals you have
been set, responding to
constraints and limitations

**Extrinsically
motivated:**
- you respond to the
  expectations of
  others
- you are less
  creative with low
  motivation

↑

sluggish
You do what you are told
(when the boss is looking)

Controlled

**(Higher levels normally include the levels below, eg a
proactive worker works when the boss is looking)**

Levels of motivation

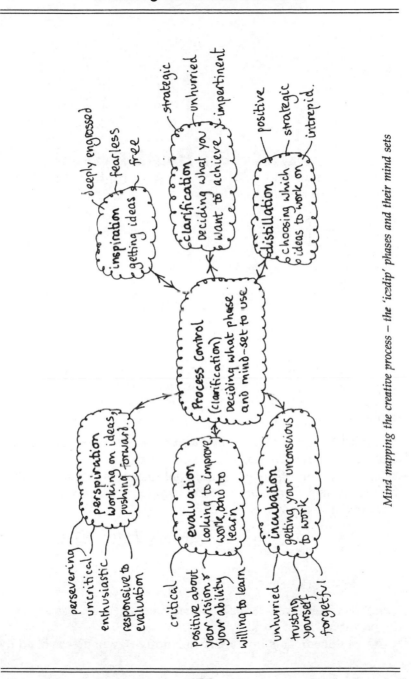

Mind mapping the creative process – the 'icedip' phases and their mind sets

FURTHER READING

RESEARCH AND ACADEMIC BOOKS

Maslow, Abraham (1954) *Motivation and Personality*, HarperCollins, London.

One of the greatest books of the twentieth century. Self-actualisation explained and put in the context of human motivation, along with its relation to creativity, and so very much more.

Maslow, Abraham (1971) *The Farther Reaches of Human Nature*, Penguin Arkana, London.

This has more detail on self-actualisation and creativity than *Motivation and Personality* but less context than the classic text. An extraordinary book.

Sternberg, Robert (ed) (1988) *The Nature of Creativity*, Cambridge University Press, Cambridge.

This reviews the academic research on creativity, including Amabile's work below.

Amabile, Teresa M (1983) *The Social Psychology of Creativity*, Springer-Verlag, New York.

Amply documents how extrinsic motives, whether evoked by

evaluation, social approval or expectation of material rewards, tend to inhibit creativity.

GENERAL BOOKS

de Bono, Edward (1992) *Serious Creativity*, HarperCollins, London.
There are very many other books by the same author, but this one summarises his ideas on tools for creativity. It focuses mainly on idea generation.

Koestler, Arthur (1964) *The Act of Creation*, Arkana, London.
An interesting read around the nature of scientific and artistic creativity. Insightful and often quoted.

O'Connor, Joseph and Seymour, John (1990) *Introducing Neuro-Linguistic Programming*, Mandala, London.
A readable text on 'NLP'. For insight into self-belief and how to get out of emotional ruts.

Russell, Bertrand (1935) *In Praise of Idleness* and (1956) *How I Write*, an essay in *Portraits from Memory*, Routledge, London.
In Praise of Idleness is a brilliant essay on values and the meaning of life. Witty, surprising and true.

Bradbury, Andrew (1997) *NLP for Business Success*, Kogan Page, London.

Ceserani, Jonne and Greatwood, Peter of Synectics (1995) *Innovation and Creativity*, Kogan Page, London.

Kinsey Goman, Carol (1989) *Creative Thinking in Business*, Kogan Page, London.

Lehmkuhl, Dorothy and Cotter Lamping, Dolores (1995) *Organizing for the Creative Person*, Kogan Page, London.

ART AND CREATIVITY

Tolstoy, Leo (1930) *What is Art?* (out of print but available from libraries), Oxford University Press, Oxford.
   This short book is a must for anyone thinking seriously about the meaning of artistic work. Passionate, clear and astonishing.

Best, David (1992) *The Rationality of Feeling: Understanding the Arts in Education*, Falmer Press, London.
Though not an easy read, and education focused, this gives an interesting slant on the ultimate purposes of the arts.

Petty, Geoffrey (1993) *Teaching Today: A Practical Guide*, Stanley Thornes, Cheltenham.
Contains a chapter on encouraging students to use the **icedip** creative process.

Also, of course, read the history of, and criticism in, your artistic discipline.

INDEX